GEOGRAPHY

of

THE SOUL

Gethsemane. Cana. Emmaus.
You'll discover the spiritual
significance of each as
you explore the...

GEOGRAPHY
of
THE SOUL

C. Welton Gaddy

BROADMAN
& HOLMAN
PUBLISHERS

Nashville, Tennessee

4253-74
0-8054-5374-1

Dewey Decimal Classification: 242.64
Subject Heading: DEVOTIONAL LITERATURE
Library of Congress Card Catalog Number: 94-9665

Library of Congress Cataloging-in-Publication Data

Gaddy, C. Welton.
    Geography of the soul: meditations on the places Jesus walked/by C. Welton Gaddy
        p. cm.
    ISBN 0-8054-5374-1
    1. Jesus Christ — Journeys — Meditations.   2. Bible N.T. Gospels —
Geography.
    3. Christian life — Meditations.   I. Title
    BT303.9.G34   1994
    232.9'01 — dc20

                                                    94-9665
                                                    CIP

CONTENTS

ACKNOWLEDGMENTS

S EVERAL YEARS AGO, WHEN I began work on this project, I experienced excitement born of an assumption that I was on to something unique. I did not recall having heard or read material elaborating a spiritual geography. I actually thought that I was engaged in a new pursuit relating geography and spirituality. Now, I know better.

Looking back, I realize that I have benefited from the ideas of people whose names I cannot call, if I ever knew them. And I am increasingly aware of other writers currently publishing a variety of perspectives on the meaning of place (or places) in people's lives.

For these reasons, I am hesitant to write this section of acknowledgments. I fear that I will fail to name influences on my work and cite sources of research which merit notation, especially some which became a part of my thought in a second–hand manner and made such an integral place for themselves in my convictions so long ago that over the years I claimed them as my own. But, for the same reasons, I am eager to acknowledge the sources of my information, influences on my thought, and encouragers of my spirit whom I can readily and pleasurably identify.

Alfred Edersheim's classic work *The Life and Times of Jesus*[1] and *The Interpreter's Dictionary of the Bible,*[2] edited by George A. Buttrick, have been invaluable sources of information on the various geographical sites discussed in this volume. Edersheim, in particular, enabled me to envision the detailed characteristics of places as remote from me in time as in space.

Through their kindness and generosity, my good friends, Mary D. and F. Howard Walsh, provided a way for my family and me to visit and to enjoy together many of the places discussed on the following pages. That unforgettable physical journey proved invaluable in the development of this narrative on a spiritual pilgrimage.

My colleagues in ministry, Don and Cathe Nixon, as well as members of the community of faith along with whom we serve, Northminster Church in Monroe, Louisiana, encouraged me to write, affirming this work as a vital dimension of our congregation's mission. Without this encouragement, the joy which I find in writing could quickly be replaced by frustration if not an outright burden. D. H. Clark and Ron Stewart, two soulmates within the Northminster fellowship, have graciously provided me with excellent word processing equipment on which to compose.

My wife Judy and our two sons, James and John Paul, continue to offer much-needed support during my wrestling matches with ideas and my mining expeditions in search of the right words with which to express those ideas. I know I can count on the substantive care of these three individuals, though I never take their care for granted or think of any one of them without love and gratitude.

INTRODUCTION

R EADING THE BIBLE OFTEN makes me uneasy. Lines of demarcation between the past and the present fade imperceptibly. History and theology become autobiography. Especially is this the case when surveying the gospel accounts of the life and ministry of Jesus.

There is a ring of familiarity in the declarations and questions set before Jesus by the people who surrounded Him on His journeys. *Are those my words?* I wonder. *Probably not,* I think, *though they could have been, because I certainly have wrestled enough with the very same issues.* Scanning the crowds attracted by Jesus' presence, from time to time I think I see my face. I am almost sure that I recognize a number of my contemporaries amid the throngs.

These sensations cause me nervously to shuffle my feet. A sickening feeling attacks my stomach, quickly recedes, and then comes again. *I am getting more than I bargained for by reading the Bible,* I tell myself. *Honestly, I am not at all sure that I want to be this involved with the gospel narratives.*

Where Jesus was seems like where I am. I know the places well. Though I am confident that everything about the biblical situation is different from my situation, much is the same.

People's names, characters' clothing, and details of the landscape are inconsequential. What is important are the experiences identified, the emotions released, the ideas shared, the dilemmas discussed, the problems addressed, and the resources promised. The significance of the various places is an extremely personal matter—for Jesus and for me.

Physically walking where Jesus walked can be inspirational. Many people find great joy traveling through Israel. Some claim a strengthened faith as the result of visiting the locales of most importance in the life of Jesus. *Just think, two thousand years ago Jesus was right here!* I have known that pleasure.

But I do not live in the past. My most basic spiritual needs reside in the present. More important to me than learning where Jesus *was* is knowing where Jesus *is*.

Visiting Bethlehem, Nazareth, or Jerusalem may feed a soul immediately, but it cannot satisfy a soul permanently. After all, what makes a place holy? Can any one spot on earth have more sanctity than another? No. Holiness is a gift from God. Sanctity is a derivative of the Spirit of God. Neither is a matter of land.

Of what spiritual importance is it that Jesus appeared in Bethlehem, Cana, and Capernaum if He cannot appear in Moscow, Tokyo, San Francisco, and Atlanta? Or anywhere I am? As I read the Gospels and discover where Jesus *was*, I look at my life and see where Jesus *is*. The two are one and the same. Jesus walks where I walk. I walk where Jesus walked.

Gethsemane is a special place not because it is Gethsemane but because it is the spot where the Son of God spent several crucial hours agonizing in prayer. Golgotha never would have been endowed with spiritual significance had not the Messiah from God died there. Here is great promise: Any place can take on uncommon importance if it is the site of an encounter with the Christ. The real holy land is the substance of a human soul—the spiritual experiences, the composite character, of an individual created in the image of God, who is holy beyond measure.

Not only does Jesus show up at a carpenter's bench and in a synagogue in Nazareth, He also comes to where I work and worship. He understands my grief while standing beside a grave prepared for a family member who died in Paris, Tennessee, because one day He stood weeping at the tomb which held the body of His good friend Lazarus who died in Bethany. Finding a seat in a graffiti-decorated subway car in New York brings to mind climbing atop a donkey to be jostled down the danger–plagued road to Jericho. It is a matter of geography— not a geography of time or place, but a geography of the soul.

I invite you to join me on a spiritual pilgrimage. The places are extremely well known. Each stop, though far away and in the past, is surprisingly nearby in the present.

The journey is personal, even intimate, in nature. So I will use the first person pronoun singular as I write about this trip. However, the pilgrimage is by no means mine alone. Thus, I will employ the second and third person pronouns (singular and plural) as well. *You* will be involved as a fellow traveler. *We* can go places together.

A word of caution is in order. At several stops along our journey—in the wilderness, at Bethany, and in the Garden of Gethsemane particularly—I must speculate on thoughts which may have filled the mind of Jesus. Determining the content of such speculation is neither difficult nor risky from the standpoint of humankind. At one time or another, virtually every one of us has stood or sat or knelt at a place where we struggled to answer such life–shaping questions as "Am I doing what God wants done? What is God saying to me through this experience? Why doesn't God intervene in history and spare us some of our pain?" How we respond to these kinds of inquiries is an important indicator of the level of our spiritual lives.

But, when we think of Jesus struggling with these same difficult questions, we tend to flinch immediately or perhaps even to deny that He ever had to resolve such thoughts. Often at tough moments in the life of Jesus—times of strenuous self–examination and reflection on the divine will—we are tempted to ignore the humanity of Jesus and to focus entirely on the divinity of Jesus. "But He would have always known God's will," we say, "Why would Jesus need any confirmation from God? He was God incarnate." However, the Bible—the Gospels particularly—do not allow us to succumb to that temptation.

Jesus was fully human. And, as a human being, Jesus experienced the wrestling matches with convictions and the struggle with profound questions which form such an integral part of our plights. Jesus also was the Word made flesh, the incarnation of God. The tension created by affirming both of these truths is a tough one to handle—the tension which must allow the completely human Jesus to raise questions and contemplate thoughts which the divine Jesus should not have had to face. But we dare not seek to alleviate that tension, to relax it even minimally. In that tension is great promise. The places where we live, work, struggle, and pray are familiar sites to Jesus. He knew such places well. Jesus is our savior in places of struggle, questions, and uncertainties even as in places of assurance, ease, and celebration.

As I embark on this literary venture retracing the steps of Jesus and seeking to take you along with me, I find myself remembering Geoffrey O'Hara's old piece of music, "I Walked

Today Where Jesus Walked." Though I have not always been fond of the melody, I like the text of O'Hara's work. His words speak to me.

I would like for you to have something of the same sense of identification with Jesus' journey that is captured in O'Hara's song and conveyed through it—with one exception. O'Hara's text concludes, "I walked today where Jesus walked and felt His presence there." My hope is that at least a few of you who read this will set the book aside with the confession, "I walked today where Jesus walked and felt His presence *here*."

Good journey. Godspeed!

PART I

A Place of Birth and Growth

1

BETHLEHEM:
A PLACE OF PROMISE

... Jesus was born in Bethlehem of Judea ...
— Matthew 2:1

PEOPLE WHO LIKE SURPRISES love Bethlehem. This little Near Eastern city is full of surprises. Be careful about approaching Bethlehem with stereotyped images and prejudiced ideas, though—either the historical one in Judea or the spiritual one in every person. Surprises come in all shapes and sizes—some attractive and some ugly, maybe even repulsive; some good and some bad. Such are the surprises encountered in Bethlehem.

Actually, the city's name provides an insight into its nature. For the most part, ancient Palestine consisted of dangerously rugged expanses of land. Arid temperatures scorched the soil. Blowing sand collected into dunes which lined cavernous cracks in the parched earth. Vegetation was scarce, virtually non–existent, as was water. To describe topographical variations in Palestine generally meant little more than distinguishing between a bad stretch of earth and an area which was even worse. But Bethlehem was different, very different. The name itself means "house of bread" or "house of food."

Travelers approaching Bethlehem for the first time must have rubbed their eyes in excitement, seeking to be sure their vision was not playing tricks on them. Beautiful wheat fields filled the valleys which stretched beneath the two rises on which the city sat. Lush terraced vineyards lined the slopes ascending to Bethlehem. Homegrown figs and olives abounded. What a surprise. Right in the middle of what seemed to be an endless expanse of ugly wasteland the beauty of fertility appeared. A sense of abandonment gave way to feelings of security. Imagine to what proportions the ancients' amazement would have increased had they known the whole story about Bethlehem and realized that from an out–of–the–way back street in this "house of bread" would come the Bread of Life and ultimate security.

Every birth is filled with promise, and so every birthplace is a place of promise—but none more than Bethlehem.

A PLACE IN TIME

Talk of the "good old days" filled the air in Bethlehem. No wonder. Even a mention of Bethlehem caused many people to think of King David. So intimate was the connection between the two that Bethlehem had come to be known as the City of David. This most–beloved king of Israel came from Bethlehem. Not only that, it was in Bethlehem that Samuel anointed David, consecrating him to God's service. What a past!

Memory plays strange tricks on people. For most individuals, a recall of the close association between Bethlehem and David evoked positive thoughts and prompted thanksgiving to God. Jewish nationalists continued to be grateful for this marvelous ruler widely respected as "a man after God's own heart." Little was said about David's adulterous relationship with Bathsheba and his instigation of a murderous plot to get rid of her husband.

Given the public's propensity for gossip and condemnation, David's hero status is somewhat surprising. Citizens prized and praised Bethlehem as the home place of this great sovereign rather than disdained it as the birth site of just another corrupt politician. Prophets declared that the long–awaited Messiah would be a direct descendant of this regal sinner–saint—and He would come from Bethlehem. David's home would be the birthplace of the Messiah.

That was good news for the people who lived in Bethlehem, but it is even better news for us. God did not give up on Bethlehem or David. God does not give up on us. Even a site where evil has ruled can be used by God in the birthing of incredible good. Time and time again divine forgiveness has swept clean the ugly clutter of a landscape, and divine grace has erected there structures of mercy.

God can take a place—whether in a person or in a nation––in which conspiracy, deceit, and other immoralities have run rampant and to everybody's amazement transform that site into a perfect birthplace for the Savior. Anyone who questions that assertion needs only to look at Bethlehem—or at himself.

No part of any individual's life lies beyond the reach of God's redemptive work. What the past holds—regardless of the sin in it—does not ultimately matter. God can fill any present with meaning and every future with hope. God visits the Bethlehems of our lives and while there creates a home for the Christ.

Not everybody looked over their shoulders when thinking about Bethlehem. The city's name caused some folks to peer into the future. At least a few people argued that Bethlehem's greatest days lay ahead of it, not behind it. Respected prophets promised that the city would host royalty once more—not the potentates of a foreign government, but the Messiah of the sovereign God. Great goodness!

Some residents of Bethlehem could not stop talking about what God had done in this place in the past. Others could not be quiet regarding what God would do here in the future. How easy to understand. In the Bethlehem of our souls we fluctuate back and forth between thoughts that the best of life is behind us and hopes that the future will be better than anything has ever been.

What about the present? Often people in Bethlehem completely overlooked the present. Not God, though.

While devotees of the past fanned the flames of nostalgia ("We will never again know the kind of glory days which accompanied David's rule.") and students of prophecy meticulously calculated the exact moment in which Bethlehem's glorious future would begin ("God will return to Bethlehem one day soon."), God filled the present with unfathomable meaning. "The Word became flesh" (John 1:14). A Savior was born—in Bethlehem!

We know the place—Bethlehem—if not by the topography and history of the Palestinian city, at least by the geography of our souls. Bethlehem is that place in our spirits where exercising faith today seems less significant than talking about what faith was like yesterday or what faith can be tomorrow. Bethlehem is that spot where God surprises everybody by entering

12

the present and endowing the immediate moment with profound spiritual meaning. Bethlehem is that place where people discover it is not more righteous to live in the past or in the future than in the present. Bethlehem is where Emmanuel appears and all who see Him with the eyes of faith learn that God is with us. Now! Bethlehem is the birthplace of Jesus.

A PLACE OF THE UNEXPECTED

Bethlehem is not particularly a religious city, at least not in the sense that most people think about religion. Prior to the birth of Jesus, virtually no one thought of Bethlehem as a holy place. Just the opposite really. Most folks associated Bethlehem with government and politics. Herod lived there. Tax collectors and census takers worked there. Not by the farthest stretch of the imagination could a trip to Bethlehem qualify as a spiritual pilgrimage. Then, as now, many people—even people of faith--saw only a minimal, almost negligible, relationship between faith and politics or taxes.

Apart from a scant reference or two in the Old Testament, Bethlehem had nothing to commend it as the birthplace of the Messiah. To be honest, one may wonder why God would have any interest at all in this center of government—a pagan one at that. Jerusalem was a different story. The holy city was a natural for earth–shaking religious events, but not Bethlehem. Bethlehem was way down the road from Jerusalem—five or six miles by actual measurement, much farther than that in personal experience.

God's ultimate revelation of the divine nature began to unfold in Bethlehem—a secular city dominated by governmental interests. If that were not a big enough surprise, look *where* in Bethlehem Jesus was born.

Herod's majestic palace towered over all of the other buildings in Bethlehem—by far the most impressive structure in the region. Its size communicated authority and its grandiose beauty intimated the power of its owner and the significance of his decisions. For years, people had looked for God's Messiah to take the government upon His shoulders, implement a major shift in power, and elevate the nation of Israel to a new plateau of political sovereignty. Herod's palace seemed to be the only place in town worthy of the Messiah's entrance into history.

However, you never can tell where God will show up. No area of life, just as no aspect of our lives, is exempted from God's interest or presence. God cares about transactions in the centers of government as well as about rituals in religious headquarters. God is just as likely to take up residence in a stable as in a palace, to rest the Messiah in a manger as to set Him on a throne.

Christ is encountered by a cradle or by a grave. To meet Christ anywhere and to be made new by Christ is to experience Bethlehem everywhere. The words which accompany an encounter with Christ can range from our exclamation, "What a beautiful baby" to Jesus' declaration of forgiveness and commission to service, "Go and sin no more."

A PLACE OF SURPRISE

A Bethlehem resides in every person's soul—a place where God enters life, whether or not we have a spot reserved for that purpose. Age and experience do not matter. Stained glass or rough-hewn pews make no difference. The only non–negotiable is the presence of Christ. In fact, the promise of Bethlehem is derived from the presence of Christ in Bethlehem, the presence of the Christ who can be met in Bethlehem.

Familiarity can be a real problem for people eager to experience the promise of Bethlehem. The place reeks with familiarity—especially to people of faith. If not the terrain and its structures, at least the name of the city seems all too common.

Oh, we know Bethlehem. It is not the kind of place in which God takes up residence. Bethlehem is as common as an old shoe. We know it like we know the backs of our hands. Bethlehem is where we ponder decisions, brood over failures, set priorities, evaluate dreams, plan meals, study for exams, prepare for work.

Watch out. The real promise of Bethlehem springs from the advent of the unexpected among the totally predictable, the arrival of a gift from God where everything seems to depend upon the accomplishments of people, the potential for spiritual fulfillment being discovered amid the humdrum routines of life. Bethlehem may appear common. But the promise of the place is anything but common.

A word of warning is in order. The promise of Bethlehem is not always realized exactly as we expect. Jesus, by far the most memorable person ever to be born in Bethlehem, failed to meet most of the high expectations popularly associated with the Messiah. Jesus disappointed a great number of persons who had predicted the precise manner in which the Messianic promise would be fulfilled.

The masses looked forward to the Messiah identifying himself as a mighty warrior and elevating the nation of Israel to the pinnacle of political superiority. Jesus refused to live by the sword and defined greatness in terms of humility. Religious prognosticators said that the Messiah would perform an array of miracles and impress people into loyalty to Him. Jesus rejected belief developed in reaction to miraculous events alone and sought the kind of personal devotion which comes only from the heart. Pragmatic populists pointed to the Messiah as an economic deliverer who would humble the rich, empower the poor, and turn stones into bread or do whatever else it took to see that everyone had enough to eat. Jesus dismissed a ministry of fiscal and physical satisfaction, which is temporary, opting instead to introduce people to a spiritual fulfillment which would last forever.

Frankly, even a brief stay in Bethlehem makes some folks uncomfortable. What happens there can be disturbing. Preconceived images of God shatter in encounters with the truth about God which comes by way of divine revelation. Personal biases wilt under the warm substance of God's will. Narrow prejudices snap when the universal compassion of God is seen.

The same surprise which prompts personal discomfort can also be filled with spiritual promise. Thanks be to God! What so many people would gladly settle for in Bethlehem falls far short of what can transpire in this place. In the first century, when Jesus was born in Bethlehem, people did not get what they wanted. Instead, they got more than anyone ever imagined could realistically be expected. It is no different today.

Any journey to Bethlehem should be taken with care. In that holy spot where Jesus is born, we may have to give up prejudices, fears, traditions, and expectations that are as comfortable for us as they are destructive to us. Such a change packs a wallop—a jolt to our souls—even if it is best for us. Bad ideas do not die any less painfully than do good ones.

In the midst of the discomfort of giving up what should be set aside, though, suddenly the wonder of God among us surprises us. God is among us! The promise of Bethlehem is a surprise. And the surprise of Bethlehem is a promise. It was then. It is now.

2

EGYPT:
AN INTERIM PLACE

And he [Joseph] arose and took the Child [Jesus] and
His mother [Mary] by night, and departed for Egypt.
— Matthew 2:14

E GYPT IS A PLACE WHERE people go when they
originally intended to go somewhere else. It is a second
choice in travel plans, not a place where travelers wish
to take up residence and spend a lifetime. Egypt is a spot where
people stay only until they can move on to the site which had
been their first choice as a destination.

From the earliest moments of His infancy, Jesus attracted
controversy and lived under an imminent threat of danger, life
ending danger. No sooner did the civil sovereign whose realm
included Bethlehem hear of the birth of Jesus, a baby rumored

to be a potential king, than he issued orders for an execution of infant sons in this little village. Herod would tolerate no rivals. He cared little for how many lives had to be destroyed in order to make him feel secure.

Herod did not make idle threats. Though he was unusually generous with his subjects, the king possessed a paranoid suspicion which made him mean. Joseph likely knew that Herod had killed three of his own sons. Most people were aware that Herod had ordered the execution of one member of each family in his kingdom at the time of his burial to assure proper mourning in the land. When Joseph learned of the king's plot aimed at getting rid of Jesus, he immediately made plans to get out of Bethlehem.

At first sound or sight, Egypt seems like a place far away from Bethlehem. In terms of physical geography, it can be, but not necessarily. When it comes to spiritual geography, Egypt is closer to Bethlehem than most of us think.

When Jesus was born, the territory of Egypt embraced the Siniatic Peninsula, which lay only a short distance from Bethlehem. Perhaps Joseph took his young family there. Though close to Bethlehem physically, politically the region of Sinai extended beyond the control of Herod. Gaza was across the border. A place of much-needed retreat and security is often closer and more accessible than people imagine.

However, the territory of Egypt stretched all across the northeastern part of Africa, with breezes from the Mediterranean cooling the land in the north and hot winds from the desert scorching everything in the south. So Joseph may have taken his family on a lengthy journey hundreds of miles down the Nile. One legend places Joseph, Mary, and Jesus in a town called Matariyah, which was located northeast of Cairo. Other ancient sources put the three in Babylon, Romgarious (the site of modern Cairo), and Hermopolis Magna (a town in the middle of Egypt). When safety is a concern, the distance to safety seems almost irrelevant.

A PLACE OF COMMON SENSE

Most of us identify with Egypt more than the other sites in Jesus' childhood. Stormy blasts suddenly rush into our lives and threaten our wellbeing. We look for time away, a place to retreat both physically and spiritually.

Today a holding pattern is as common in people's lives as it is around a busy airport. Scores of individuals who are ready, even eager, to get on with their lives confront situations which send them to Egypt. In Egypt, life is "on hold."

Common sense takes people to Egypt. For some strange reason, people have difficulty identifying sound reasoning, common sense, as the gift from God which it is.

Undoubtedly Joseph felt torn. His livelihood was tied to a carpentry shop in Nazareth, and he had a responsibility to provide for his family. But Jesus' safety could not be ignored, not when Herod was talking of a slaughter of infants. So questions swirled around in Joseph's mind: *Does it make sense to pick up this newborn Child and move Him and His mother to Egypt? If this were only an ordinary situation, I would know what to do, but this is different. Isn't Jesus a holy Child? Will God not protect Jesus from all adversity? Why should I worry about the safety of One sent from God? If one's mission is holy, is not safety guaranteed?*

Faced by difficult situations, confusion is not uncommon. A young man who has sensed God's call to ministry wrestles with a decision over whether or not to take time for preparation or merely to launch out on his own, trusting that God will equip him along the way. A missionary who has served in one location for a decade suddenly faces the possibility of deportation, or worse, because of the success of a political coups d'etat in the government of the land. She ponders whether to continue her work or to back away for a while and allow the explosive nature of the situation to be defused. A business woman faces a major challenge which could cost her a job. She knows she is right and the challenge is wrong. Should she tackle the challenge immediately or pull back and wait for the challenge to self–destruct?

Though situations vary, the most disturbing questions within these situations remain pretty much the same: Can it ever be pleasing to God for urgent responsibilities to be delayed? Should we not always attack evil immediately and forthrightly? Does Christianity have within it any provision for escape? Or is escape always to be equated with spiritual cowardice? If the cause is right, will not God always protect us even if we act with less knowledge than is desirable?

The issue is obedience to God. Is it more holy to follow the counsel of common sense or to act in opposition to what conventional wisdom demands? Can reason serve faith? Are practical thoughts gifts from God or temptations leading away from compliance with the divine will?

Joseph viewed a decision to get away from the irrational, murderous policies of Herod by taking his family into Egypt as both practically and spiritually sound. Thankfully, this carpenter from Nazareth realized that often the dictates of common sense and the directives of God's will are the same. How a person views the value of common sense in the face of a major challenge often determines the spiritual value (or lack of it) of that person's life after the crisis has passed. Using our intellectual resources is not a denial of faith. Acting impractically is not more spiritually courageous than behaving practically. God offers reason as a good gift, encourages actions based on a responsible exercise of wisdom, and sanctifies the practical with holiness.

A PLACE OF WAITING

Egypt is a place of waiting, and that is the problem. Few people like to wait for anything, much less for something as crucial as doing God's work.

Sense the situation on the boundary of Egypt. Jesus has been born "in the fullness of time." At last, the hope of the ages has arrived. God is ready to get on with the redemption of humankind. Why should a mad, unreligious king be allowed to send Jesus on a detour? Should not Joseph flaunt his courage and go on back to Nazareth? What Jesus has to do is far too important to risk a period of waiting, even though He is an infant.

This is familiar. We know this Egypt place, and we have struggled with decisions about whether or not to go there. Egypt is a place of waiting. And we don't like to wait—for anybody or for anything.

Some people travel to Egypt of their own free will. A young couple is eager to get married. They can hardly wait to live together. But both lovers agree that a period of waiting is needed—to get to know each other better, to receive marital counseling, to establish a stronger foundation for a home. So they delay the date for their wedding.

A Christian politician is finally ready to run for public office. He has so much that he wants to accomplish that the sooner he can get at it, the better off he will be. At least he thinks that way initially. Then, a poll among voters indicates that his chances of being elected are slim this year. A board of advisers agrees. The man decides to wait for a more promising time to throw his hat into the ring.

Not everybody is so fortunate. Many people make their journey to Egypt against their wills. A college student eager to graduate and go to work in a family business is placed on academic probation. A man in the prime of his career, on the verge of a major breakthrough in sales, becomes the victim of a hostile corporate takeover and loses his job. A couple ready to embark upon their longtime dream for retirement years receives word that the report on a recent biopsy on the woman is being delayed for further study.

For some reason, certain individuals view waiting—especially forced waiting—as weak, unspiritual, and nonproductive. That is not the case at all. A stay in Egypt can be productive, strengthening, and religiously enriching.

A suddenly unemployed man waiting for another job develops a clearer understanding of security, what is most important in life, where his greatest loyalties should lie, and how to trust in God's care. A hospitalized woman, frustrated by the havoc which a broken leg played with her travel plans, learns the spiritual discipline of patience and discovers how closeness to God can be nurtured in stillness. A man taking an experimental drug for his illness realizes dimensions of trust and hope in God which he never would have known had his life had no delays.

A PLACE OF DISTRACTIONS

Egypt, at least the one in the soul, is not a place to which people generally want to go and stay, for several reasons.

Egypt is a place of allurements, distractions, and temptations. The political situation in Egypt was not a lot better than the political climate was in Bethlehem of Judea; it was just safer for Joseph, Mary, and Jesus. Egypt was not without a dark side, though.

Most folks associated Egypt with sorcery, witchcraft, and magic. Jesus' enemies, later in His life, slandered Him for having spent time in Egypt. They spread rumors that, as an illegitimate child, Jesus grew up in Egypt learning magic and performing the kind of tricks which eventually came to be regarded as miracles.

Jesus' enemies lied about Him. However, they did correctly understand Egypt as a place where a person could take a wrong turn, follow a path which led away from God, and pick up habits and loyalties which have no place in the life of a person devoted to God. You have to be very careful in Egypt. Though this spot is a place of retreat from threatening situations, it is not outside the providence of God. Fundamental commitments are not abrogated during a period of waiting.

Then, too, Egypt is often a lonely place—at least it may be at first.

Such was not the situation for Joseph, Mary, and Jesus. Many Jews from Palestine had sought refuge in Egypt for one reason or another. In fact, the influx of Jewish people into Egypt had been so significant that every city in Egypt had a colony of Jews within it. The city of Alexandria was home for more than one million Jews. So Joseph and his family likely found a warm and ready welcome in this strange land.

Unfortunately, that is not the case for everybody. Some individuals have to make their way into Egypt completely ignorant of the lay of the land and unfamiliar with anyone who inhabits it.

To be forced to relocate where you do not want to be and to retreat when you desire to gain the offensive are bad enough in themselves. Having to accept either plight alone is even worse.

No wonder people do not like to stay long in Egypt. But how do you know when to depart, when to go home again? Egypt is also a place for developing sensitivity to God's time. The God who accompanies people into Egypt is the God who will lead them out of Egypt—if they will only stay sensitive to God's leadership. God's time is unique. God's clock strikes when our timepieces remain silent. The moment to depart from Egypt is the second when God signals the time for an exodus is at hand. What is on our personal agendas for that hour, like the reading on our watches and the dates on our calendars, really does not matter. As soon as God beckons us, we had best go. Joseph did, taking Mary and Jesus with him. In Egypt wise people nurture their sensitivity to God's leadership so as not to miss the summons sounded in the striking of God's clock.

The Egypt in our souls abounds with spiritual meaning. Even during a short stay in this place, a person learns of the comprehensiveness of God's care. God's compassion has no boundaries. God is in Egypt even as in Judea.

God is the great deliverer. God delivered Jesus from the bloodthirsty reach of king Herod and then delivered Jesus from confinement in the strange land of Egypt.

God abides with people in the delays of life as well as in life's busiest moments. More than that, at times, God inspires delays.

To be sure, Egypt is an interim place—a place where some people do not want to go at all and a place to which others go only for a time. There is more to life, more to the spiritual journey, than Egypt. But if this spot in the soul is not visited at some point, life can be tragically and needlessly cut short. Life can be devoid of the dimension of profound spiritual meaning which can be discovered only in Egypt.

3

NAZARETH:
A HOME PLACE

. . . Jesus came from Nazareth in Galilee . . .
— Mark 1:9

THERE'S NO PLACE LIKE HOME. Some people spit out those words with stinging sarcasm, harboring bad impressions of home. Other folks make the same statement with a softness and sincerity born of intense appreciation, if not outright love, for their homes. What happens to an individual in the place called home impacts what happens in that individual's life everywhere else.

Nazareth was the home place of Jesus. During Jesus' boyhood, Nazareth was about as insignificant and non-descript as a place could be and still be named. The little village had developed in the hill country fifteen miles from the Sea of Galilee. Distances and directions really did not matter, though, because Nazareth, which was not on a main road, seemed like a long way from everywhere else. Visitors arrived there intentionally; no one just happened by. Most people passed Nazareth at a distance, not even aware that they were close to a village.

Why would anyone want to live in Nazareth? The village was immanently forgettable—historically as insignificant as it was physically remote. Most everybody's homesite has at least one claim to fame—a battle which was fought there, a major accomplishment by some of its citizens, a famous person who was born there. Not Nazareth. Not a single reference to Nazareth can be found in any of the ancient non–Christian literature, in the Jewish Talmud, or even in the published works of Josephus, the Jewish historian who seemed to write about everybody and everything.

Eking out a living in Nazareth was a sizable chore. Water was scarce. The village had only one spring. Industry of any kind was almost non–existent. Even if Nazareth had produced a commodity to export, getting that item to potential buyers would have proven extremely difficult. Consequently, almost all of the residents of Nazareth worked for the Roman oppressors who had occupied Galilee and now ruled it. We can only speculate how the Nazarenes must have hated working for superiors whom they resented and thus how the citizenry was gripped by oppression.

People who did not live in Nazareth knew little about the place. Those outsiders who knew anything at all about the village knew they did not like it. Comments about Nazareth ranged from ridiculing jokes to serious condemnations. Nazareth was a "wrong-side-of-the-tracks" kind of place. But it was home for Jesus.

With effort Jesus could have become conscious of and even pondered the larger world from Nazareth. The mountainous ridge on which Nazareth was perched, 1650 feet above sea level, provided a panoramic view of the Sea of Galilee and of two great caravan routes in the region—one to Damascus and Baghdad on the east and one to Caesarea toward the west. Did Jesus regularly climb to this area of high ground and spend time watching the traffic of commerce below, speculating about the destinations of the caravans and wondering about the needs of the people involved? Of course, we do not know, but it would be no surprise if that were the case. Every home provides a perspective from which to view the rest of the world, if a person wants to find it and take advantage of it.

A Place of Fellowship

Everybody has a home place—physically or spiritually—of growth and life or of stagnation and death. To get at the exact nature of an individual's home place is often difficult, however. Home is an emotional concept as well as a geographical location. Seldom can a person speak about home rationally and objectively. Home touches our emotions.

Home is a spot in a person's soul as well as a space on a map. It is a place to which we go or for which we search when we need understanding and support, nurture and comfort, counsel and enlightenment, or maybe only rest. Tragically, some people never find their home—internally or externally. When that happens, those people's lives are worse off because of the lack of that discovery. Other folks find their home and do not want ever to leave it again. Home can be tricky that way—an elusive place to some, a captive place to others.

At its best, home is a place associated with fellowship, nurture, love, respect, and growth—growth "in wisdom and in stature, and in favor with God and man" (Luke 2:52). Given its somewhat deprived nature, how did Nazareth ever fill such a bill for Jesus? It did so in the same way in which any other place can serve as a home for anyone else—by supporting people who prize their togetherness as a caring family and who nurture a strong awareness of the presence of God in their midst.

Nazareth's greatest gift to Jesus was Mary and Joseph. The home place of Jesus was a poor little village constructed as best people could manage on a high spot of rugged terrain in Galilee. The home place of Jesus was a small shelter in which to sleep, eat, and relate and a cramped carpenter's shop in which to hone God–given skills. But that is only a tiny part of the story. Home for Jesus meant loving relationships with other people, relationships which aided His personal growth and sensitized Him to the importance of meaningful communication with God.

Undoubtedly, Jesus' thoughts of home called up the scent of recently cut wood, the feel of a splinter sunk deep into His hand, and an awareness of people who cared for Him whether He was working or playing, laughing or crying. Home really is much more than a structure in which to live; it is a place of the heart.

A PLACE OF LEARNING

Nazareth was the place where Jesus learned the history of the Jewish faith, studied the Holy Scriptures, and heard the challenge of God's call to service. Likely, the religious education of Jesus began before He could talk. Every pious Jewish family vowed to train each of their children to recognize God as Creator and Father—from the time the child was a baby in swaddling clothes.

Watching His mother Mary's regular activities was an education in itself—a religious education. Every week Mary prepared the Sabbath meal, lit the Sabbath lamp, and organized the household for its observance of a day of rest and worship. Long before He understood exactly why or how, Jesus sensed the importance of God in the life of His family and participated in the family's primal activity of worship.

Once Jesus was old enough to speak, various sights within the family's house surely prompted Him to ask spiritually–significant questions: "What is that thing on the doorpost and why is it there?" "Why does Mother wear that parchment around her arm?"

Joseph happily would have explained to Jesus that a *Mezuzah* had been placed by the door of their residence in conformity with the teaching of Deuteronomy 6:9. A folded copy of the *Shema*—"Hear O Israel, the Lord our God is one Lord and you shall love the Lord your God with all your heart, and with all your soul, and with all your might" (Deut. 6:4)—was placed in the *Mezuzah* in a manner which allowed the divine name to be seen. As people moved into and out of the house, they touched the doorpost ornament out of reverence and then in devotion kissed the fingers of their hand which had been placed on the name of God.

Likewise Mary would have taken great pride in talking to Jesus about the phylacteries which people wore when they prayed, sometimes as bands on their hands and often on their arms as bracelets. As His mother explained to Jesus how words from the *Shema* (Deut 6:4) were placed in the containers which people strapped around their heads or arms, she could take advantage of another opportunity to stress the importance of this fundamental religious law.

The first prayers which Jesus ever heard probably were voiced in His home. In the very rooms in which He daily ate, slept, and interacted with other family members, Jesus experienced the joyous celebrations of holy days—the remembrance of Israel's deliverance from slavery in Egypt, an anniversary of the cleansing of the temple, a period of thanksgiving for the annual harvest. And Jesus was no mere spectator. Children were assigned important responsibilities in the home–based rituals of Judaism.

At the age of five or six, Jesus began His formal education in Nazareth. Sometimes in the open air and more often in the synagogue, Jesus listened to scholars read, interpret, and explain the Bible, beginning with the book of Leviticus. Later, when He reached the age of ten, teachers introduced Jesus to the book which contained the traditional laws of the Jewish people—the Mishnah.

Home for Jesus was a place of God–consciousness. Home can be, and should be, such a place for us as well—starting now if it has not been that for us in the past.

Each of the crucial religious educational experiences in Jesus' early life occurred in the home. It did not matter that the home was poor and small, not rich and spacious. Spiritual nurture does not depend on physical structure. As a matter of fact, even if a household is breathtakingly beautiful, it fails as a home unless spiritual nurture is one of the gifts of love shared among the people who live there.

A PLACE OF GROWTH

Ideally, home is a place where children begin to grow and adults keep on growing. To be sure, that is not always the case. It was not for Jesus. Siblings and friends with whom Jesus played as a child harshly disassociated themselves from Him once He began to behave as an adult. Even Mary, the mother of Jesus, had her share of problems accepting the nature of the ministry to which Jesus gave Himself after He left home. Though she and Joseph had prayed constantly for spiritual sensitivity and strict obedience to God's will in the life of Jesus, moments came when Mary wanted to rescue Jesus from the life–threatening controversy caused by His conformity to God's leadership.

As a child Jesus attended the synagogue faithfully—going to school there on week days and participating in public worship services there every Sabbath day. When Jesus began His public ministry, He made His way to the synagogue just as He had done hundreds of times before. However, when, as a part of the synagogue's worship, Jesus read from the scroll of Isaiah and identified Himself as the one anointed by God to carry out the ministry envisioned by that ancient prophet, other members of the synagogue turned on Him. People who had pampered and encouraged Jesus as a child suddenly wanted to literally kill Him.

Home is a place where public compassion for a child can be transformed into public rejection when that child becomes an adult—especially if that hometown boy or girl dares to make a commitment to living as God's servant. Too many people think they know too much. "Oh, we remember you when you danced in the street. You grew up here just like the rest of us; who do you think you are?" Such a person may serve well elsewhere. As Jesus Himself observed, "A prophet is without honor in His own country" (Mark 6:4).

Most people learn the ambivalent nature of hometown experiences the hard way. They go home, or at least try to go home, to taste earlier happiness or to recapture feelings of glad satisfaction, only to discover heartaches. A lot of people conclude, "You can't go home again." Really, though, you can!

A person can go home again. Oh, few, if any, can return to their growing–up places, their family homesites, or their hometowns and find everything just as it was earlier. Streets change. Old buildings get torn down and new buildings are erected. Longtime friends die. New families move into the neighborhood. Babies are born. Come to think about it, for a home place not to change would spell disaster. So, if going home again means rediscovering a replica of the past, that's out. No one can go home again in that sense. But we can go home again.

If home is a place of nurture, a spot where we learned to handle both affirmation and criticism, a locale in which our minds were enlightened, our spirits lifted, and our devotion to God developed, then we can go to this place again; in fact, we need to go to this place again. Maybe we can no longer walk down some familiar street and find the old house in which we grew up or enter the city of our youth and immediately meet someone whom we know, but we can—and must—locate home within our souls. If we cannot return home, we will do well to carry our home with us.

Nazareth, like your home or mine, may not seem like much to anybody who did not grow up there. It is so very common. But for those who did grow up there, common or not, appreciated or scorned by others, Nazareth is home. And everybody's home is a place of importance—whether it is Nazareth or another town or a spot on the terrain of our souls, a spot to which we love to go, breathe its familiar air, and prop up our spirits in it for a while.

There really is no place like home.

PART II

A Place of Work and Ministry

4

JORDAN RIVER: A PLACE OF COMMITMENT

. . . Jesus arrived from Galilee at the Jordan . . .
— Matthew 3:13

THE ONLY WAY TO REALLY enjoy the Jordan River is to get into it, to get sopping wet. As you splash around in the Jordan, you may understand the significance of this grand river in the history of the holy land.

The swift current of the Jordan washing against your body can prompt you to recall Moses as he stood on the banks of this body of water. You can almost feel his longing to cross this final barrier to the promised land. Only those early escapees from Egypt who got wet in the Jordan knew the joy and freedom of a new home.

More often than not, the promised land lies on the other side of the Jordan. Entering into the land of new hopes requires getting across the Jordan. There is no way around it; you can only go through it.

The Jordan River flows rapidly down a segment of the Great African Rift, twisting and turning its way to the Dead Sea. Jesus was baptized there, and He began His public ministry there. Each of us also has a Jordan in our souls. Most people step, or leap, into the currents of the Jordan on their way to maturity.

Jesus traveled willfully, and willingly, to the Jordan River. This sometimes swampy, papyrus–filled river was a stop He wanted to make before proceeding with a ministry which would hold few opportunities for stops. But his interest was not the scenery or even the water.

Jesus was about to begin a public ministry of redemption, the mission of God, a task for which He had come. While He hacked away at piece after piece of wood in his father's carpenter shop and carefully smoothed the rough-cut edges of a new table, no doubt Jesus pondered the larger world and questioned how the good news of God's reign could best be shared. Once Jesus knew the time had come for Him to initiate a public ministry, He looked for a way to demonstrate before other people His intention to serve God completely.

The preaching of John the Baptist along the banks of the Jordan River was akin to an alarm clock. When Jesus heard that the Baptizer was in the region heralding a message of preparation for the coming kingdom of God and administering a baptism of repentance, He knew the kingdom of God was at hand. Jesus knew it; though, as far as we know, up until this point, He had not said it aloud. Jesus wanted to meet John the Baptist and begin His public mission.

Jesus' baptism perplexes some people. The baptism of John was an immersion of repentance—a public declaration of a turn–around in a person's life, a visual dramatization of the decision to pursue the will of God with all of one's being. Jesus was already doing the latter and did not need to do the former. Jesus had no sin screaming for forgiveness. Every day of his life had been devoted to embodying God's will. Why would Jesus want to get wet in the Jordan?

PLACE OF IDENTIFICATION

Jesus carried out his ministry as an insider—a savior who rubbed shoulders with those to be saved; a healer unafraid to be in touch with people who were ill; a rabbi eager to sit among students; an advocate of righteousness who saw his place among sinners. People respond to individuals who understand their plights and share in their needs. Sensitive to this reality, Jesus identified with all whom He would seek to serve.

The Jordan River was the place to start—a place of identification. People were flocking to the Jordan River to hear John the Baptist preach. Many of these people, an astounding number really, were responding to the prophet's summons for them to experience a baptism of repentance. What better site for the public ministry of Jesus to begin! These were people with whom Jesus desired to identify—people for whom He held a genuine love. Being baptized in the Jordan River by John the Baptist was one way Jesus could identify with the people to whom He would minister, the people with whom He would serve God.

At the Jordan River place in our souls—which cannot be ignored spiritually—we often balk at getting in the water. Especially is that the case when time in the Jordan is associated with an act of identification. A rationale for abstinence develops whether or not it is ever spoken: *I don't want to have anything to do with those people. Maybe it sounds bad to say, but I'm better than they are. If I identify with them, even to minister to them, others may misunderstand. Why, others might think I'm no better than these folks I'm trying to help. I don't want that.*

Jesus could have put forth such an argument for staying dry in the presence of John the Baptist. After all, in responding to John's call to a baptism of repentance, Jesus ran the risk of people seeing Him as a sinner in need of salvation. Those other people at the Jordan River had no way of knowing Jesus' baptism was different from theirs—motivated by a desire for identification, not by a need for forgiveness. But Jesus took that risk, the first of many risks which filled His ministry.

A Place of Submission

When Jesus waded into the waters of the Jordan River, He saw far more than a wild–looking prophet clothed in camel hair standing in midstream and scores of anxious people milling around on the shoreline. If, for Jesus, the Jordan River was a place for identification with other people—the people to whom He would offer redemption—it also was a place of submission in His relationship to God—the One making Him the Redeemer. My, how all people could benefit from regular visits to the Jordan place in our souls.

What person has not found herself in a quandary over the matter of submission to God? A young college graduate has planned carefully for a career as a fabric buyer for a major department store. Ready to proceed with her first job interview, this lady cannot shake a growing sense that God is calling her into some form of missions in the international community. What should she do—proceed with her own plans or submit to what seems to be God's plan? An agricultural specialist has looked forward to his retirement as a time for relaxation, reading, and fishing. At long last, his final month on the job is at hand. However, yesterday's mail brought an invitation for this man to spend the next six months in a hunger–ridden, underdeveloped nation helping farmers to increase the productivity of their food crops. Suddenly his carefully–thought–out intentions seem to clash with God's commission. What should he do? These two individuals and countless others like them stand poised on the bank of the Jordan River. What they will do next, whether or not they will enter the water for baptism, is for each of them a dilemma of submission to God.

We do not know whether or not Jesus struggled before accepting God's call to a public ministry. He could have. As a boy of twelve Jesus talked with certainty about doing God's work. But years later, though still unalterably dedicated to carrying out God's will, Jesus questioned if His work had to be done exactly God's way—by means of a cross (see Matt. 26:39-42). If Jesus did struggle with the divine will, coming to the Jordan to begin His ministry must have been for Him an act akin to drinking the cup—"let this cup pass from Me"—for the first time. If, on the other hand, Jesus experienced no struggle regarding His ministry, His entrance into the Jordan would have been a joyful, long–and–eagerly–awaited act of submission to God. *Finally, I can take action on the submissive devotion to God which has been a part of my life for as long as I can remember.* At the Jordan, submission can occur either way or with elements of both options present.

Submission to God is not a spectator activity. The religious significance of the Jordan River cannot be realized from shore.

Submitting to God's will involves moving into the depths, stepping more by faith than by sight. It is strange, though, that the somewhat weak and shaky faith which causes a person to put her first trembling foot into the water tends to grow stronger and more secure the deeper into the water that individual goes. Obviously, it is not the water that makes a difference. It is the confidence which comes with complete submission to God.

A PLACE OF COMMITMENT

Another name for all that happened to Jesus at the Jordan River is commitment. Jesus' identification with humankind and His submission to God clearly showed His commitment to live in obedience to God. The Jordan River is a place of commitment.

Beliefs can bring an individual to the Jordan but beliefs alone can not assure that a person will get into the waters of the Jordan to be baptized. Not even biblically–based, theologically–sound beliefs can assure immersion in the Jordan. Emotions, even spiritually–oriented emotions, are equally inept at this point, as are logical thoughts. Only commitment will suffice. Commitment alone causes an individual to enter the waters of the Jordan River as an act of devotion to God.

At the Jordan, we have to either put up or shut up. The Jordan is not a spot for making long speeches about our beliefs or for reciting historical creeds of faith. It is a place for action. The Jordan is a site where demonstrations of beliefs must replace declarations of beliefs, or everybody might as well go somewhere else.

Feelings involve the heart. Thoughts spring from the mind. Beliefs, one means by which people respond to revelations from God, arise out of a mixture of thoughts and feelings.

Commitment, another and a more important means by which people respond to revelations from God, requires more. Commitment is an act of the total person. Commitment is an intentional act in which an individual stakes all of life on what is felt, thought, and believed. What is remembered about Jesus' visit to the Jordan is what He *did* there—not what He *thought, felt,* or *believed* there. For Jesus, the Jordan River was a place of commitment.

It is for us as well. The Jordan River is that spot on the landscape of our souls where we take a risk of faith, stake our lives on what we believe to be right and true, and unconditionally set the direction in which, with God's help, we intend to move for the rest of our lives.

A foxhole in the midst of battle or a cell in the county jail, an altar of a worship center or a chair in our office can be the site where we arrive at the Jordan River. Water may be present nowhere, but in our souls we are standing up to our necks in the rushing current of the Jordan. And the question before us is a question of commitment.

According to the stage dramatization of Sir Thomas More's life, the Tower of London was a Jordan River kind of place for him. While serving as lord chancellor in the English government, More refused to support his king's battle with the church. The king was seeking the church's permission to divorce his wife so he could marry another woman. Thomas More's elevation of personal conscience over secular authority sent the king into a rage. Subsequently More was imprisoned as a prelude to execution.

More's family members were distraught. During one of their visits with him in the Tower of London, More's wife and daughter pleaded with him to bend his convictions a bit, to give in to the political sovereign's wishes enough to save his life.

Neither saw their requests as unreasonable or severely detrimental.

Sir Thomas More, this prisoner of integrity, "a man for all seasons," explained to his daughter that when a person makes a commitment, he holds himself in his hands like water. If that person opens his hands then, More went on to say, he need never hope to find himself again. A person who cannot make a commitment is devoid of self-respect and unable ever to know the best meaning of life.

At the Jordan River, deciding about commitment was not a matter of holding Himself in His hands like water for Jesus. Jesus was in the water. The challenge for this would–be savior was whether to stay in the water or to get out. Jesus had arrived at a moment of decision—a pivotal experience in His life in which He had to exhibit His commitment to God's will or get out of the water, quickly dry off, scurry back to Nazareth, and get busy in His father's carpentry shop. It is difficult to imagine what we would have lost had Jesus not been able to make a commitment. But He was. And He did. We have a savior!

When John the Baptist lifted Jesus' body out of the watery tomb into which he had lowered it, Jesus was on His way to being whoever God called Him to be and to doing whatever God called Him to do—no turning back. A commitment had been made. An unconditional commitment, which, in reality, is the only kind of commitment worthy of the name.

A PLACE OF CONFIRMATION

For Jesus, the Jordan River was also a place of confirmation. He perhaps neither knew nor expected this benefit when He went to the Jordan. Not everyone experiences confirmation there. But how grateful Jesus was for this surprise.

Jesus traveled to the Jordan River aware of what He needed to do. And He did it with no contingencies, with no promises, with no assurances. Jesus did not submit to baptism in the waters of the Jordan in order to experience a blessing from God. Not at all. Jesus entered the current of the river seeking nothing other than obedience to God, which is in itself a blessing.

While standing in the waters of the Jordan River, though, Jesus heard the voice of God declaring, "This is my Son, the Beloved, with whom I am well pleased" (Matt. 3:17). Affirmation. Encouragement. Confirmation. Commission. What a surge of joy and a rush of energy must have raced through Jesus.

Had Jesus not gone into the water, would He have heard the voice? We only can guess at an answer to that question. The circumstances do make us wonder, though, what signs from God we are not seeing and what words from God we are not hearing because we are unwilling to wade into the Jordan in our souls!

This much is sure: Confirmation from God does not come apart from submission to God—not for Jesus and not for us. The Jordan River is that spiritual landmark where people make life–altering decisions about obedience to God. For that very reason, not every individual experiences the Jordan River in the same manner.

Almost everybody arrives at the Jordan River at one time or another. Some individuals simply get wet there. Others identify with people who need them, submit themselves to God, and hear the voice of God expressing pleasure with their lives. They get wet too. When these people emerge from the water, however, the most important evidence of their visit to the Jordan is not streaks, splotches, and drops of water which can be quickly toweled off, but spiritual qualities of life which no amount of rubbing can ever remove from the soul.

The commitment which finds expression at the Jordan is strong in intention and singular in focus, though complex in its sources and multi-faceted in its meaning. For Jesus, the Jordan was a place of identification, submission, commitment, and confirmation. For us, the Jordan place in the soul may be far more than that. But it is not very likely that the Jordan will ever be less than that.

5

THE WILDERNESS:
A LONELY PLACE

. . . Jesus was led up by the Spirit into the wilderness . . .
— Matthew 4:1

I HATE THE WILDERNESS. Sometimes, when I want to be alone may find it acceptable, but even then I quickly tire of the desolation and desire to move on. I prefer solitude in a more comfortable place. I do not like loneliness anywhere. The wilderness is ugly—physically unattractive and emotionally disturbing. It frightens me.

While standing in the Jordan River, you can be completely oblivious to the wilderness—even to the rest of the world actually. However, only a short distance from the river is a rather scary place designated in the Scriptures by a variety of names—wilderness, desert, lonely place.

Immediately after He submitted to the baptism of John in the Jordan, Jesus went to the desert. The Gospels tell us that the Spirit led Jesus into the wilderness. Whether or not that is how most people get to the wilderness, I am not sure. But we all, at one time or another, find ourselves in the wilderness.

One can hardly go anywhere in life without having to pass through the wilderness. The length of a person's stay there may vary, but what happens in the wilderness directly affects who that person is and what that person does everywhere else the person goes.

The geographical wilderness into which Jesus moved consisted of a thirty–five-by-fifteen-mile stretch of land between Jerusalem and the Dead Sea. Nothing about it was attractive—nothing. One visitor to this place described it in terms of yellow sand, crumbling limestone, and scattered shingle. Warped and twisted ridges run first in one direction and then in another with no discernible pattern. Jagged rocks and contorted strata stand out against dusty hills and blistered, peeling limestone. Close to the Dead Sea, the wilderness contains dangerous precipices that drop off dramatically and crags in which an unsuspecting traveler can lose his life. [1]

Heat pounds the hardened, cracked surface of the wilderness, reflects off the rugged terrain, and threatens to suffocate those who spend any extended time there. The searing heat blasts into a person's face from above and below. The sun burns the skin and empties the sweat glands to a point of dehydration. Simmering, shimmering waves of heat rise from earth to disturb the body and trouble the mind.

That is the wilderness to which Jesus went. Old Testament writers called it, *Jeshimmon*. The place could not have been given a better name, for *Jeshimmon* means "the devastation."

A LONELY PLACE

Not all wildernesses look alike. Some are wooded rather than barren, cold instead of hot, moist rather than arid, cramped instead of expansive. Regardless of the temperature, humidity, and ground cover, a wilderness is a wilderness—a dangerous place, a disturbing place, a place of struggle, a place of temptation. And what makes all that worse, every wilderness is a lonely place.

When a person visits the wilderness of the soul, external circumstances matter little. Aridness may characterize an individual's spirit rather than the land. Rugged may describe chaotic emotions rather than rocks. A person—like Jesus—can be surrounded by other people, even be the focal point of a crowd—as when Jesus was crucified—and still feel completely alone and can cry out, "My God, my God, why hast thou forsaken me?" (Mark 15:34).

One individual may find the wilderness in the reception room of a psychiatrist's suite, while another experiences desolation amid the noisy activities of an unemployment office. Some folks enter the desert without ever leaving home. Others create a desert everywhere they go.

A wise counselor described the personal wilderness which all people visit as our "inner world," the as yet "unexplored and uncharted region" of our very selves. This author depicted life at the wilderness place in the soul: "Picture yourself as having a private inner world all your own and as getting 'lost' in your own thoughts . . . turning over choices and decisions, and the feelings you have about those choices and feelings." He warned that these thoughts keep a person awake at night or fill an individual's dreams should sleep occur. "You are trying to work out *what* you think, *what* you are going to do, and *why* you think and do what you decide." [2]

A PLACE OF QUESTIONS

Questions dominate the wilderness—relentless, nagging, de-manding–to–be–answered–immediately inquiries. Questions are as numerous as the sharp–edged rocks which cut our feet and the hot grains of sand which blow into our faces. No area of life is off-limits to rapid–fire interrogation: *What am I going to do with my life? Do I want to succeed at all costs or risk failure? How should I define success? What are my goals? What are my wants and needs; and how do they differ from each other, if they differ at all? How important to me are the opinions of other people, especially other people's opinions about me? To whom will I listen? What great wrong have I done to bring on this period of testing? Is God punishing me or seeking to guide me?*

Convictions threaten to wilt and die, under the relentless pressure of a wilderness struggle. Ideas and assurances which seemed so stable at the Jordan River suddenly shake as if in a violent desert storm—a soul quake. Doubts rush in with a force which threatens to bowl over faith. A person in a spiritual desert must answer questions he never imagined he would even raise. *Has God really called me to a task, or have I been the victim of auto–suggestion? Does God literally summon people to service? Did I experience God's blessing at the Jordan River, or was I so intent on hearing from God that I created what I needed? In light of the way things have changed, can I make a deal with God—that I will obey God completely if God will ease up on a few of the divine demands? Can I renegotiate commitment? Do I actually want to spend the remainder of my life trying to serve people who at any moment can turn on me?*

Night is no better than day in the wilderness. Maybe worse. Sunset brings a dramatic drop in temperature. Chill bumps replace beads of sweat. The encroaching darkness envelopes the soul as well as the land. Strange noises sound louder—and closer. Loneliness grows deeper. Rest refuses to arrive.

Day and night Jesus weighed the meaning of His identity and wrestled with the tension between His humanity and His divinity. Perhaps He also weighed various options regarding the nature of His ministry. *What am I doing here? Am I not the son of Mary and Joseph who belongs in a carpenter's shop? But am I not also the Son of God charged with a mission to the world? How should I do this? Am I not powerful enough to do as I please—to win people's loyalty by force if they refuse to follow Me freely in faith? What would be so wrong with that, if it is for their own good? Who are the models to which I should give attention——Elijah, one of the Maccabees, Herod, the suffering servant described by Isaiah? Should I choose courses of action which are popular and sure to gain a large following, or should I conform to the promptings of God and risk having only a limited number of true disciples?*

We know; my, how well we all know. Though we cannot identify even slightly with the Messianic consciousness in Jesus, we regularly battle decisions about our identities and how we should best express them. *How can God use me? At one moment I feel like the most important person on earth, and the next I feel lower than the lowest form of life. And the repetitious plunge from the former to the latter is wearing me out. What should I do? Should I be more aggressive or passive, active or reflective? Or, does it even matter? Can I take the consequences of being honest about who I am and what God is calling me to do? Can I endure the criticism—and maybe more—sure to result from my support of controversial causes?*

A PLACE OF TEMPTATION

Temptation! That is what all of this is—the staggering questions, vacillating convictions, attractive illusions, and disturbing delusions. The wilderness is a place of temptation—mentally unsettling, emotionally rattling, spiritually discomforting, physically depleting temptation.

Knowing you are in a wilderness does not make coping with that place any easier. Similarly, recognizing temptation (one's situation) offers no assurance of overcoming temptation. Jesus struggled with temptation in a lonely place, a wilderness.

The experience is familiar to most of us, as is the place. We battle temptations daily. And, regardless of where we are when a war with temptation breaks out, we feel as if we are alone.

Our temptations rarely involve the kind of history–altering consequences associated with the temptations which Jesus faced. While He may have struggled with the means of His Messianic ministry, we may struggle with temptations related to the use of time, the morality of a sales technique guaranteed to double our income, the treatment of a family member in trouble, or responsible expressions of our sexuality. Though our resolution of a particular temptation experience will not affect the possibility of salvation for all people, our decision will impact directly the quality of our lives and the nature of our faith.

Seldom do temptations offer clear–cut alternatives from which to choose. Values swirl and intermingle like blowing sand in a strong gust of wind. More often than not, temptations force people to determine a course of action from among options which range between what is good and what is best. In fact, sometimes the issues become so confused that individuals lose sight of whether they are confronting evil, arguing with God, talking to themselves, or engaging in some of all of that.

If only the temptation place were not such a lonely place! But it is—always. Battling temptation is solitary work. No person, regardless of how close or caring, can resolve another person's struggle with temptation.

The Spirit led Jesus to the wilderness where He sought direction for His public ministry. At the Jordan He had heard God's affirmation of Him as the Son of God. But, how does the Son of God live in this world? What would be the distinguishing marks of His mission? Would He live the way other people expected or God's way?

At the core of Jesus' temptation experience was the issue of trust—trust in God. That, by the way, is the bottom-line concern in every person's struggle with temptation. The challenge of trust is as tough as it is common. Even for a person who has decided to do God's will, the discernment of God's will is seldom easy.

Jesus had to confront whether He would be the kind of Messiah everyone would appreciate or whether He would follow a course of ministry charted by the ancient prophet Isaiah. Isaiah's vision centered on selfless service and suffering. On the other hand, if Jesus turned stones into bread, word about His power would spread quickly. Who wants to be hungry? Without question, people would flock to His side heralding Him as an economic savior who could put food on every table. Jesus would be praised as the master of the quick fix. People would follow Him in droves.

Every day we find ourselves in dilemmas—wildernesses—in which we can purchase loyalty rather than earn it, adopt business methods which will improve the economy at the expense of morality, live for public approval rather than function with personal integrity—and thereby promote ourselves. In other words, we can decide to spend our lives serving ourselves, or we can choose to serve God.

Then there was the temptation of power. Jesus had been charged with announcing the advent of God's reign, divinely commissioned to bring people into alignment with God's purposes. He could do that slowly, patiently, and lovingly—accepting the risk of failure inherent in such a non–manipulative method. Or He could turn to a use of power that would assure compliance and success quickly. Why not the latter? If He brought people under God's command, would it make a difference how He did it?

In the wilderness, compassion and ambition often get so entangled that one cannot be distinguished from the other. Add the lure of success and a real danger develops. When ambition prevails, people discard all interests in competence. They give priority to control, sacrifice gaining personal respect for establishing the authority of a position, set aside compassion to engage in intimidation, and allow the ends to justify the means in decision–making. Love dies.

Who does not struggle with the lure of power as Jesus did? Acting as a power–broker seems so much more preferable than serving as a minister. Forcing compliance with our wills appears far more attractive than granting people the freedom to accept our plans of their own accord. Brandishing a law is so much easier than practicing grace. We know very well that our culture bows before power with an admiration which unselfish love seems unable to attract. The same was true in the culture which surrounded Jesus.

Surely, Jesus' struggle with temptation reached its peak as He was asked to consider whether or not He was an exception––different from every other person and exempt from the laws of nature. *Why, surely,* the voise of evil alluringly chided, *as the Son of God, You can leap from the pinnacle of the temple without bodily harm. What a display that would be. People will run over each other trying to support a person who can accomplish such a feat. Everybody will listen to You and accept Your teachings. Who wouldn't want to be a disciple of a man who can exploit the spectacular!*

Jesus knew better though. In the first place, religious convictions and spiritual dedication do not begin in the eyes. Seldom does what a person sees determine what that person believes. People who would follow Jesus because of His ability to do great miracles would always be wanting to see one more miracle as a condition for continuing their interest in Him. More important than that, however, Jesus had identified with all of humankind at the Jordan River. He was not about to renege on that identification while in the wilderness. Jesus resolved that if He was to become a part of people's lives, He would enter with love at the beckon of their hearts, not come crashing in as the result of some spectacular leap from a high place.

How real and powerful this same temptation is to most people who have found the wilderness spot in their souls. A tendency to see ourselves as exceptions is almost inevitable: *That law does not apply to me. I am an exception to the general rule. I can be unfaithful to my wife and nobody will be hurt. I can cheat on my IRS forms and no one will ever know. I can abuse my body with ceaseless work and unrelenting stress without affecting my health. I am different. It won't happen to me. I can live without God.*

If we do not take control of this mentality in the wilderness and completely set aside the destructive idea that we are different from everyone else, exempt from the normal consequences of behavior, the truth soon stops us in our tracks. How much like everyone else we are! Not uncommonly, the lesson comes laced with disillusionment, tragedy, defeat, and incredible hurt.

A PLACE OF PRAYER

The wilderness is a place of temptation; that is the downside of this spot. The upside of it is that the wilderness is also a place of resolution—a spot where temptation can be defeated and direction decided—because the wilderness is a place of prayer.

After forty days, Jesus left the wilderness which covered the land not far from the Jordan River. However, Jesus regularly sought a lonely place in which to pray.

Repeatedly the gospel writers mention times when Jesus broke away from the crowds and even from the disciples to be alone. He had to have His moments alone with God if He was to serve God faithfully amid the press of other people. Jesus' ability to renounce temptations and to overcome evil in public related directly to His capacity to keep times alone for private prayer and for nurture of the strength which comes only from God.

Jesus' excursions to a lonely place for prayer kept Him fit for the horrendous battles with temptation which hounded Him until He took His last breath on the cross. Enticements to give up ministry as a suffering servant and to take up the identity of a military hero, a magician, or a governmental leader never ceased. The crowds pleaded for it. Even the disciples were ready for a different approach.

Nowhere else and at no other time was the value of Jesus' solitary experiences of prayer any more apparent than amid the chaos and temptations of Golgotha. His enemies, part of the crucifixion crowd, taunted Jesus to display His power by coming down from the cross if He really was the Son of God. It must have seemed like being back in the wilderness again. Surely Jesus must have wanted to show them, to prove them wrong, to humble them. Their taunts could have penetrated to the core of His being just like the challenges to turn stones into bread and to jump from the pinnacle of the temple had done. Thank God for the regularly kept solitary moments of prayer in which prior commitments had been strengthened and reassurance realized. Jesus lived to serve God. He would die that way as well. So, from the cross, Jesus rejected yet another temptation and sighed, "Father, into Thy hands I commend my spirit!" (Luke 23:46).

One final observation: According to the Gospel of Mark, during His stay in the wilderness immediately after His baptism, Jesus encountered both angels and wild beasts. Anybody who has experienced the wilderness of the soul understands that comment. Thinking back about times I have spent in the wilderness, images of angels and beasts almost always appear in my memories. In fact, not only do I see them, they are so familiar that I know their names.

6

CANA:
A PLACE OF
CELEBRATION

. . . there was a wedding at Cana in Galilee . . .
Jesus . . . was invited. . .
— John 2:1–2

L ISTEN. SOUNDS OF JOY reverberate across the community. The conversations are indistinguishable, but the happy spirit of the talk is unmistakable. Occasional shouts of elation and sudden bursts of laughter rise above the steady hum of enjoyment. Strains of music waft in and out. A celebration is underway, and Jesus is in the middle of it.

The occasion is a wedding ceremony. The location is Cana of Galilee, a little village nine miles north of Nazareth. But celebration knows no geographical restrictions. Festivity frequently breaks out when Jesus shows up. The place is inconsequential. A human soul can ascend to lofty heights of joy at a birthday party in a family residence or during a worship service in a sanctuary, with friends around a picnic table or before an officer of the law who grants a driver's license to a young person just turned sixteen.

Cana was not the kind of place people automatically associated with festivity. Far from it. Among first century folks who knew the site, any mention of Cana as a fun place would have produced a cynical laugh.

The village of Cana was lodged on the slope of a windblown hill surrounded by minimally productive fields. It was as drab as it was small. The dwellings in Cana, such as they were, were set precariously on a series of terraces. About the only claim to fame which Cana could muster was its pomegranates—the best in Palestine a lot of people thought. Other than that, not much could be said about Cana. The word "festivity" would not have come to mind. Likely, people would have associated Cana with poverty.

Be that as it may, on the day Jesus visited Cana, the village hosted a celebration which continues to be discussed almost two thousand years after the fact. A wedding was quite an occasion for Jewish people. The marriage day of a couple symbolized God's union with Israel. Little wonder the place of the wedding was decorated so lavishly. Myrtle branches, torches, flowers, and lamps set on top of poles adorned the approach to the site of the wedding ceremony. Music accompanied the traditional pilgrimage which brought the bride and the groom together.

A wedding was a big deal for Jewish people. In the thought of Judaism, the marriage day of a couple symbolized God's union with Israel. Little wonder the place of the wedding was decorated so lavishly. In the house of the ceremony, greenery and budding plants lined the court and covered the gallery which opened into the room chosen for the wedding feast. Lamps and large candlesticks cast an elegant glow across the people lounging around the table covered with good food. Huge water pots for ritual washings could be seen, as well as the various containers of wine, a drink necessary for a Jewish wedding.

A wedding day in Cana, poor though it was, assured everyone of a good day, a pretty scene, a festive moment, a place of celebration. Honestly, though, what the wedding day celebration in Cana turned out to be cannot even be compared with what it would have been had Jesus not been there.

That is true of most Canas, of all places of festivity. Jesus brings to a place—whether in Palestine or in a person's soul—a quality of joy which prompts singing and laughing that would be merely perfunctory without His presence.

A PLACE OF JOY

Some interpreters of Scripture suggest that Jesus only went to Cana to appease Mary, His mother. These folks have trouble acknowledging that Jesus would seek out a party. Unfortunately, their attitude is an all–too–common one.

Many people—a surprising number, in fact—cannot imagine Jesus laughing. The very thought of a fun–loving Messiah strikes them as spiritually revolting. A few noted theologians even contend that a holy place has no room for laughter. To such people, somber attitudes appear more righteous than joy. Scowls seem most appropriate for services of divine worship. Smiles are spiritually suspect. Unfortunately H. L. Menchen described innumerable individuals with his characterization of the spirit of Puritanism. They have "that haunting feeling that somewhere, some place, somebody is happy." [1]

A person who views life primarily in negative terms and suspects any evidence of happiness is not likely to understand God as the author of hilarity or accept Jesus as a model of good humor. That person will not like Cana. An individual's understanding of God tends to incline that person to health or sickness. Thus, if the divine image in an individual's mind is negative in nature, that person extols unhappiness. In turn, that joyless lifestyle reinforces a concept of God devoid of laughter. Though difficult to believe, some fanatical religionists in the past actually sought to pass laws prohibiting laughter on the Lord's Day.

The New Testament tells us that Jesus expressed His joy audibly. Every one of His beatitudes begins with a word of happiness. Jesus spoke of laughter resounding in heaven when a sinner repents on earth. Surely Jesus laughed aloud when He sat with His disciples delighting in their nightly fellowship meals, when He employed a humorous hyperbole while telling a favorite parable, when little children played at His feet and climbed onto His lap, when a formerly blind man whose eyes had been opened danced around in a celebration of sight, and when He saw the happiness of His friends after He raised Lazarus from the dead. Jesus must have laughed. And it all started at Cana.

Jesus journeyed to Cana and while He was there He chose to be a part of a wedding celebration. As it turned out, Jesus became more involved in the wedding festivities than He may have intended. He was not exactly the life of the party, but He certainly saved the party.

More people showed up for the wedding than the host had expected. Perhaps because of Jesus. After all, He brought some of His disciples, probably five, with Him. Whether because of these additional guests or for some other reason, during the wedding celebration, all of the wine in the household was consumed. When this happened, Mary requested her Son's assistance in providing more wine. Though, at first Jesus resisted any involvement in this situation, eventually He blessed the water available for ritual washings, six big vessels of it, and thereby produced more wine, good wine, better wine than anyone at the feast had tasted that evening.

A PLACE OF NEW BEGINNINGS

Cana was a place of new beginnings. Obviously it was that for the couple getting married there. But it was for others as well.

Skeptics probably began to criticize Jesus as soon as He appeared at the wedding party. "You never would catch John the Baptist in a place like this," some might have commented. Others took the cue. "John the Baptist understood the severity of the times. He had no interest in partying. Proclaiming God's Word and doing God's work are serious endeavors."

Such accusations were no doubt joined by persons seeking to prove a point about Jesus: "I guess this will show everybody who Jesus really is. I don't know how to explain what happened at the Jordan River, but the Son of God has better places to go than to a wedding and more important things to do than supply wine for an ill–prepared host."

People might have made such remarks to criticize Jesus, but, their words were basically honest. John the Baptist would not have attended a wedding party—or any other kind of celebration for that matter. The rough–shod, wilderness–based preacher was a somber prophet. Also, Jesus' actions at the wedding feast did in fact reveal His identity. Though He had other places to go and more important work to do, He had time to enjoy a party.

In the mind and ministry of Jesus, celebration did not stand against religion or outside it. Jesus saw a relationship between celebration and religion. Indeed, each was a part of the other.

Festivity is not an enemy of faith. The gospel is good news—really good news, almost unbelievably good news. So, naturally, joy became a vital dimension of the serious work of Jesus. Celebration dots the lives and marks the souls of people who follow Jesus, the giver of lasting joy.

A new day was dawning. A new kind of faith was emerging. Jesus was not John the Baptist. Though the two cousins lived at the same time, they were of different eras. Christianity differed from Judaism. Jesus made law—with its stringent, sometimes strident, demands—subordinate to vibrant grace. The new wine in the water pots at Cana was nothing compared to the new creation to which Jesus called the whole world. Years later, the apostle Paul captured the significance of Cana as he wrote about the impact of Christ on a person, "the old has passed away . . . the new has come" (2 Cor. 5:17).

Jesus brought joy to the party, but this was only the beginning. Before His public ministry ended, Jesus brought joy to a variety of settings, some of which seemed immune to joy. Jesus caused rejoicing from a band of lepers banned from contact with other people, from a city torn by religious controversy, and from mourners grieving in a cemetery. Anyone who experienced this new creation knew Jesus' joy. Look at the people in Cana.

Or go to Cana. Find the Cana spot in your soul.

At the spiritual Cana in a person's life, memories from the past and redemption for the present and future wait to be wed. Folks who have broken promises, betrayed trusts, compromised the truth, and practiced poor stewardship can start over at Cana. Individuals for whom religion is a burden and guilt a constant companion can find relief in Cana. They can take on a yoke which is easy and can experience mercy which breaks the bondage of guilt.

People who have blown opportunities, wasted days, and failed at major tasks will flock to Cana if they ever comprehend what can happen there. Cana is a place of new beginnings.

A PLACE OF EXTRAVAGANCE

Frequently, people who travel to Cana get more than they bargained for there. In many ways, Cana is a place of extravagance.

How much wine did Jesus make for the wedding guests? Evidently, more than enough for everybody. And how did it taste? It was the best wine that had been served all evening, by all accounts. Why the abundance? Why the excellence? Weddings were commonplace in Jewish society. A wedding in Cana could not have been that important. Why the extravagance?

Jesus' action at Cana provided an important insight into His character. He was forever doing more than had to be done. And everything Jesus produced was far better than it had to be. At Cana the subject was wine. Later the subject was life.

Jesus did not care much for minimums. That is why He had problems with legalists. Religious law forbade physical acts of murder and adultery, but Jesus affirmed a morality which prohibits raw anger and lust in the heart from which such immoral behavior arises. Traditional laws exhorted people to do their duty: If you are commanded to go a mile with a man, do it. Jesus called upon people to live by love: If you are commanded to go a mile with a man, go with him two miles. When respect for an institution prevented acts of compassion toward a needy person, Jesus commended the higher good: The Sabbath was made for people, not vice versa.

At the same time that Jesus elevated morality to new and extravagant levels, He also condemned moderate expressions of understanding and miserly forgiveness toward moral failures. Jesus called for unlimited forgiveness devoid of a hint of judgment. Rather than engage in an acceptable form of retaliation toward wrongdoers, Jesus challenged His followers to repay evil with good and to pray for those who wronged them. Justice, which represented the pinnacle of legalistic morality, was not enough for Jesus. He pleaded for a greater form of righteousness evidenced in the practice of mercy.

Repeatedly Jesus demonstrated His opposition to conformity to the lowest possible expectation. Jesus urged people to live life at its highest and fullest. And He personally embodied the substance of His challenge.

Near the end of His ministry, Jesus received an extravagant expression of love from a woman who emptied an entire vessel of costly ointment on Him. Almost everybody who witnessed the act criticized the woman and spoke of her waste. Jesus did not, though; He praised her profusely (see Matt. 26:6-13). If the critics at Bethany, that "place of reflection," had been present in this "place of celebration," they would have understood. At Bethany, just prior to the conclusion of His public ministry, Jesus praised the kind of extravagant behavior which He had practiced at Cana, as His public ministry began.

A Place of Affirmation

Cana was a place of affirmation. Probably no one said it just that way. However, almost everything which transpired during that wedding party in Cana indicated affirmation. The very presence of guests in the house affirmed the couple getting married as well as the covenant of marriage. All the sounds and sights of festivity affirmed the importance of celebration. Jesus' miraculous transformation of the water into wine affirmed the goodness and promise of God's creation.

Cana is where we go to be present with a friend who has just received a promotion. "Work is an important part of life," our presence says, "and you are to be commended for working in a manner that has brought you recognition." Cana is the gathering place for friends eager to affirm a couple's adoption of a child. Words and actions express affirmation for the new parents' love and their desire to nurture a new person.

At Cana, either by words or actions or both, we recognize an artist's creativity and affirm her expressions of a God–given talent; we let a teenager know the importance of reaching an age which allows him to drive a car alone; we congratulate a young woman who is graduating from college; we join a family as they dedicate a dwelling place to God; we eat a piece of cake with a friend on his ninetieth birthday.

Cana is a Christian place, a place where Christian affirmation is directed to people as they negotiate the various transitions, rites of passage, and periods of growth in life. Strangely, an uninformed observer at Cana cannot always tell who is being affirmed and who is doing the affirming. Everybody benefits from and delights in affirmation—both the givers and the receivers.

Not uncommonly, significant spurts of spiritual growth and a joyful acceptance of additional religious responsibilities result from the kind of affirmation which abounds in Cana. During a stopover at Cana, people tend to realize that so much more good can be accomplished and so much more evil can be avoided by means of affirmation than can ever be seen by a series of denunciations, regardless of how well intended the negatives may be.

About the only drawback to a visit to Cana is regret about what others are missing. Amid the festive celebrations in Cana, you may find yourself almost aching because so many people whom you love have not recognized the importance of visiting Cana. So many Christian pilgrims fail to recognize that Cana merits a visit from the soul. You wish that all people would realize that a trip to Cana is every bit as profound in spiritual importance as the emotional happiness sure to be experienced there.

For most people, one trip does it. Go to Cana once and experience the fulfillment of its promise as a place of festivity, and no one will ever have to urge you to go to Cana again. You will find yourself hardly able to wait until you can get there--again and again.

One time Jesus told His disciples that He had come to give life, abundant life; a richer, fuller, happier, more festive life than anyone had previously known or than anyone could ever find from another source. Cana was a case in point, an early glimpse into the awesome truthfulness of Jesus' words.

Cana hosts and inspires everything a celebration should be. I wouldn't miss it for the world!

7

CAPERNAUM: A COMMON PLACE

And when he [Jesus] had come back to Capernaum . . . it
was heard that he was at home.
— Mark 2:1

F EW PEOPLE THINK OF Capernaum in relation to
faith—except for the Gospel writers that is. Capernaum
is the only place in the gospels where Jesus was said to
be "at home." When the authors of the Gospels thought of
Capernaum, they thought of Jesus—and, thus, of faith.

What strange discontinuity—that two sets of feelings (or
thoughts) about the same place would be so different. Therein
lies the problem faced in and by Capernaum, both the one
located on the Plain of Gennesaret where it touches the
northern edge of the Sea of Galilee and the one situated

somewhere along the soulscape of every person's life, probably close to the center.

Jesus chose to base His ministry in Capernaum. For an extended period of time Jesus lived in Capernaum, ministered in Capernaum, and traveled to and from Capernaum, as He broadened the reaches of His ministry across the land.

To reside in Capernaum was to be at the center of much activity, to enjoy a sweep of beautiful scenery, and to form relationships marked by racial diversity. Capernaum was a thriving town of 15,000 citizens made up of Jews, Bedouins, Roman soldiers, and merchants from all over Mesopotamia and Egypt.

Strategically located on the Sea of Galilee as well as on the main road leading from Egypt to Damascus, Capernaum constantly hosted large numbers of tourists and a great variety of business people. Tourists stared appreciatively at the snow-capped height of Mount Hermon, visible to the north of the city. Merchants viewed row after row of sheds, heard the steady rapping of hammers, and smelled a mixture of odors from dye-works, pottery kilns, and fish cleaners.

Like any city of its size, Capernaum had more social problems than it could resolve. The town's market was noisy as well as wealthy. The highly visible presence of a garrison of foreign soldiers in Capernaum evoked resentment and frequently prompted outbursts of anger in the streets. A customs house where Roman officials exacted taxes, was often a site of great consternation.

However, Jesus liked Capernaum. He made numerous friends there—a centurion whose name we do not know and Jairus who ruled the synagogue. Jesus enlisted several of His disciples from Capernaum—Matthew, Simon, Andrew, Simon Peter, and Zebedee's sons James and John.

Evidently, Capernaum liked Jesus, too. People flocked to Jesus' side when He was there. They lined up to be healed. The crowds were so great that a few people even devised special means for gaining Jesus' attention, such as laying a paralyzed man before Him after lowering this man through the roof above Jesus.

Things changed, though. Capernaum later became the object of Jesus' scorn, the recipient of His harshest condemnation. Jesus compared Capernaum to the notoriously evil Sodom of Old Testament times, a place where a failure to take advantage of great privilege resulted in horrendous guilt. He likened the spiritual condition of Capernaum to the desolation of death. Rhetorically, Jesus asked, "And you, Capernaum, will you be exalted to heaven?" A chilling answer followed, "No, you will be brought down to Hades" (Matt. 11:23).

What happened? Over the span of only a few months, how could a place which Jesus chose as His home become a place which Jesus condemned to Hades?

A PLACE OF ROUTINES

Most of us know Capernaum better than we may wish to admit—both the ancient physical town and the contemporary spiritual spot in our beings. Capernaum is a common place.

Routines dominate life in Capernaum. People are preoccupied with establishing a home, plying a trade, going fishing, responding to civil authorities, attending the synagogue, and paying taxes. Practical matters take center stage in Capernaum—how to pay this month's bills, how to increase business, what to do about the government, why one child is maturing and another is regressing.

Then there is all the diversity of cosmopolitan Capernaum. Residents are forever caught up in trying to get along with people who are different—struggling to know when to be critical of a neighbor and when to be silent, when to reach out and when to draw back—or resolving to ignore other people and live as a hermit.

Jesus chose as the center for His ministry a place of routines, a site where one day seemed very much like every other day. Meeting the demands of each day left little time for thinking about the larger picture of life. Though probably no one said it outloud, in Capernaum practical concerns took precedence over spiritual concerns. After all, the spiritual side of life seemed so unrelated to the practical side of life anyway. Yes, Capernaum is a place in our souls.

Once the nature of Capernaum is properly understood, a person can understand as well what went wrong in Capernaum—and what can go wrong in the Capernaum of the soul!

Capernaum is a place of miracles and an ordinary place. Simultaneously, not sequentially. While everybody else was going about his or her daily business in Capernaum, Jesus began to preach the message of God's reign there, to teach the principles of a life under God's rule, and to extend healing to individuals who were broken or ill.

When word about Jesus spread across the community, people flocked to get a look at this fellow and to hear Him speak. Hurting folks sought out Jesus with requests for help. They watched Jesus and listened to Jesus—and then they went back to their routines, doing everything just as they had done before meeting Jesus. The newness of the Messiah's message and the wonder inspired by His healings only temporarily distracted the people of Capernaum from their concern with ordinary tasks. Oh, most folks enjoyed the distractions. But these people knew better than to pay so much attention to Jesus that they altered their lives. In their minds, that would be frivolous at best; at worst, dangerous. Another day's work had to be done. That's what was pressing. Their families would expect food on the table by early evening.

In Capernaum, even the people who stop what they are doing to witness a miracle from God do not allow themselves to think for one minute that the miraculous could be a regular part of their lives. Buying and selling, births and deaths, eating and sleeping—these are the rhythms of life, not miracles. Oh, a miracle might happen occasionally, but not often. Not often at all.

Tradition carries great weight in a common place. Immerse that tradition in religion and you get a near immovable phenomenon. Look at Capernaum.

People in Capernaum had practiced their religion in the local synagogue in almost exactly the same manner for as long as anybody could remember. Religious leaders did not want anyone tampering with their tradition. Neither did lay people. Religion in Capernaum was as common as everything else there. Stability provided security and comfort.

One Sabbath day in the synagogue in Capernaum, Jesus healed a man with a withered hand. His critics reacted angrily: Jesus had broken a Sabbath tradition. Though what He did was good beyond measure, Jesus' action went against what was common, and the people would not have it. An uncommon act of compassionate goodness early in His ministry sealed Jesus' fate. Mark wrote that as a result of Jesus' tradition–breaking healing in the synagogue at Capernaum, religious officials there began to plot the best way to destroy Jesus (see Mark 3:6).

The trouble in the synagogue at Capernaum was symptomatic of a more profound problem which plagued the whole city. In Capernaum, as elsewhere, Jesus brought the demands of God's rule to bear on every aspect of life. He called upon people devoted to God to live out that devotion in the marketplace, in their homes, in relation to strange soldiers, and in response to the government's demand for payments of taxes. Jesus rejected outright the idea that true religion can be relegated to one dimension or to one institution of life alone.

People in Capernaum felt very much like a woman who recently voiced a protest against her pastor's sermon on Christian social ethics. "When Christianity gets to the point that it affects my politics and finances, it has gone too far!" she exclaimed. According to the teachings of Jesus, when Christianity gets to that point, it is beginning to touch life as God intended.

In a place like Capernaum, people have a tendency to make religion common. Religion can take its rightful place alongside politics, economics, family concerns, work, and recreational pursuits. But religion is expected to remain *beside* these interests, never to pervade them or impact them—and certainly not to change them.

We know Capernaum. Dangerous reasoning goes on in this common place in our souls: *Church is fine; an important institution in the community. However, the church needs to tend to its own business and not meddle in secular concerns. Religion is private; business is public. The same rules cannot govern both. The church should stick to helping charity cases and keep quiet about housing conditions, public education, zoning laws, and city council deliberations. Those secular concerns should be off limits to the outreach of religious institutions.*

So went the reasoning at Capernaum in Jesus' day. So goes the reasoning at the Capernaum place in our souls today.

The people of Capernaum got into serious trouble with God. They wanted no part of a divinely–inspired spirituality which affected their traditions, routines, work habits, and daily lifestyles. Citizens of Capernaum had compartmentalized life. They welcomed both the holy and the common as long as each was kept in its rightful place. But the two were not to be mixed. Conversely, Jesus commended the holy amid the common place. In fact, He warned the people in Capernaum that they would either have to repent of their segmentation of life and approach every dimension of their days from the perspective of their obedience to God or that they would experience a serious demise.

The people of Capernaum obviously rejected the message of Jesus and for all practical purposes rejected Jesus himself. Subsequently they experienced the demise about which Jesus had warned them.

A PLACE OF DECEPTION

That is frightening. What happened on that seaside plot of land a long time ago can happen in a person's heart. Thus, the Capernaum place in the soul will do well to learn from the once thriving town of Capernaum which is no more.

Crowding around Jesus is not to be confused with a support for or a commitment to Jesus. Jesus encountered the most unrepentant people of His whole ministry in the very place where He drew the largest crowds and excited the most positive public interest. On one occasion, Jesus even remarked that if the people in the old town of Sodom had received as much instruction and as many opportunities for repentance, the Sodomites would have repented. What an indictment!

Looks can be deceptive. Gathering to hear Jesus teach, to watch Him work, and to request His help creates an appearance of loyalty. Beware. Standing alongside Jesus is not the same as living in obedience to Jesus.

Many of the people who tagged along after Jesus during His days in Capernaum never internalized anything He said or duplicated in their own behavior anything He did. Why they stayed with Jesus—whether out of curiosity or self-interest or for some other reason—no one can say with any assurance. Obviously, though, people in Capernaum did not stay around Christ to become Christ-like. Ironically, a majority of the residents of Jesus' home place during a critical period in His ministry turned out to have the same unrepentant, life-segmenting, faith-isolating spirit which He came to eliminate.

Then, too, it became readily apparent in Capernaum that living in close proximity to Jesus does not guarantee or suffice for an acceptance of Jesus.

Jesus was in and out of Capernaum regularly. On numerous occasions, He stayed in Capernaum for several days consecutively. You would think that people who were that close to Jesus so often would have embraced Him with their thoughts, emotions, and obedient devotion. That was not the case, though.

The same principle applies to the Capernaum in our souls. We are challenged to welcome Jesus into our lives, not just to observe Him, study Him, and talk about Him. Pondering the words and works of Jesus cannot serve as a viable substitute for implementing His words and work, for living the life to which Jesus summons all people. Similarly, watching Jesus heal or forgive others does not bring healing and forgiveness to the observer. Meditations on Jesus cannot take the place of an acceptance of Jesus.

Today's visitors to Capernaum see only ruins—impressive ruins, to be sure, but ruins nonetheless. The ancient city that Jesus knew is gone. None of its structures still stand. Nothing of the earlier promise of Capernaum remains.

The people of Capernaum did not heed the words of Jesus and repent. They never really allowed the teachings of Jesus to impact the common pursuits of their lives. So Capernaum was destroyed. More accurately stated, Capernaum destroyed itself.

Who does not know a common place in the soul? A place where routines look like ruts and boredom reigns as the sovereign emotion? A place where a shroud of familiarity covers everything so tightly that nothing appears holy? A place in which whatever religion can be found there seems as common as everything around it? This is Capernaum.

Jesus loves to live in a common place. He readily will take up residence in a Capernaum and do some of His greatest works there. But a place praised by Jesus can become a place cursed by Jesus. Everything depends upon whether or not a person responds to Him with penitence and obedience and invites Him to stay forever.

All who have eyes to see and ears to hear best see and hear—and also acknowledge and accept Jesus as Lord of the common as well as the miraculous.

8

SEA OF GALILEE: A PLACE OF TRANSITION

> . . . Jesus went away to the other side of the Sea
> of Galilee . . .
> — John 6:1

THE SEA OF GALILEE SAT like a vast bowl of water wedged between the high mountains of northern Palestine. Everyone who knew anything at all about the region of Galilee was thoroughly familiar with this popular body of water. Few landmarks stand out with more prominence in the ministry of Jesus than this heart–shaped sea.

Not everybody used the same name when speaking of this place, however. Long–term residents called it Lake Chinnereth. Other folks referred to it as the Lake of Tiberias. Those who labeled the water a lake argued that it was too small to be considered a sea. Maybe they were right. But the watery mass was big enough—seven miles wide and twelve miles long—to provide plenty of space between points on its opposite shores. And it was more than deep enough—two hundred feet in places—for a person to drown in.

Neither the size nor the name of the place mattered much, though, when compared to its significance. This expansive pool of fresh water played an important role in the lives of the people who lived around it and made excursions on it.

The Sea of Galilee was a place of play. The brilliant blue, oftentimes greenish-tinted, water invited people to come to its shores, lounge in the sun, and get wet. On a pretty day along the banks and in the shallows of the Galilean water, people gathered to enjoy beautiful scenery, unparalleled in the region, and to experience refreshment.

The sea was a virtual fish factory. Countless varieties of fish grew in this lake. Not surprisingly then, the sea was a work place. More people worked in the fishing industry than in any other business pursuit. And fishing enterprises thrived on the Sea of Galilee. The prizes of a big catch found their way onto tables for miles and miles away from the sea.

The Sea of Galilee also served as a major thoroughfare. Not only did most of the roads in Galilee lead to this particular body of water; in many instances, this water provided the best means of transportation available between the numerous important villages which had developed around it.

Jesus preached the gospel, taught details of kingdom citizenship, and healed persons in almost all of the communities which had grown up on the shores of the Sea of Galilee. Jesus regularly crossed this expanse of water in a boat. Once He even walked on it.

The Sea of Galilee provided Jesus with a much–needed means of transition. At times He traversed the waters to be with people and at other times He journeyed across the lake to get away from them.

Regardless of what we call this spot in our souls or how we feel about it or why we rush to it, a Sea-of-Galilee place exists within all of us. It is the spot to which we go when we need to get away, when life has crowded in on us to the point of suffocation, when everything has become so much trouble, when we seek something different, when we long for a change of scenery.

Transitions are a way of life. Sometimes we seek them out willingly. At other times, transitions are forced upon us. A place of transition is the location of the Sea of Galilee within a person's soul.

The motivation behind a transition is important, even spiritually important: *Am I moving to get away from a bad situation or to experience something new? Or is it some of both and maybe more? Do I believe that changing locations can get rid of these unwanted feelings within me? Are these negative emotions likely to go with me? Would I have made this move had I not gone through a divorce and lost my job? Can this time of relocation become a time of growth? Am I justified in looking forward to arriving at a new place?*

Sorting out the motivations behind each transition opens our eyes to the possibilities of redemption which we may encounter along the way. A survey of the Sea of Galilee in our souls can be extremely beneficial.

A PLACE OF WORK AND PLEASURE

A less than careful observer cannot always tell whether the Sea of Galilee is a place of work or a place of pleasure, both physically and spiritually. Distinguishing between the two is irrelevant among people who find their work to be a source of pleasure or who attack opportunities for pleasure like going to work.

At the same moment that one person meanders to the Sea of Galilee for a period of enjoyment, another may rush there out of a sense of professional duty. While one man lazily fishes for an entree for his family's evening meal, another laboriously draws in fish nets hoping to make a daily wage. You could see it all at the Sea of Galilee, a place of work and a place of play.

Not only is the Sea of Galilee a place for both work and play, it is a means of transition from work to play and from play to work. In this sense especially, the sea is crucial territory for all people. Everyone needs both.

A PLACE OF FELLOWSHIP AND SOLITUDE

Similarly, the Sea of Galilee makes possible two other situations each of which, though different from the other, is essential to a person's health. Jesus experienced this watery expanse as a place of fellowship and a place of solitude and as a way to get from one to the other.

As much as Jesus loved people, He had to have time alone. When the need for solitude developed, Jesus wisely acted to meet that need. More than once, Jesus boarded a boat which took Him to the other side of the lake and away from the crowds.

Jesus' trips across the water in pursuit of solitude were not evasions of responsibility or lapses of love—not at all. To the contrary, in every instance, Jesus' retreats constituted only a different form of responsible, loving action.

Jesus had a God–given responsibility to himself as well as to the crowds, as do all people. Each depends upon the other. Moreover, Jesus realized that unless He took time to meet His own needs, He would be unable to respond helpfully to the crowds. Finding a way to enjoy the renewal which comes in solitude was as much an indication of love as interacting with the public. Obedience to God involves self-love as well as compassion for the masses.

Solitude never developed into escape for Jesus. A boat was always waiting. The same waterway which took Jesus apart from the crowds regularly took Him back again.

A Place of Public Ministry and Private Prayer

Work and play. Solitude and fellowship. These are important means of recognizing the crucial significance of the Sea-of-Galilee spot in the soul. An absence of any one of these experiences on a regular basis diminishes the fullness of that individual's existence. But there is more.

In the experience of Jesus, the Sea of Galilee served as an avenue running between public ministry and private prayer. We have to have such a place as well. Everybody does—at least, everybody who wants to be spiritually healthy.

Jesus could engage day after day in energy expending service amid the press of large crowds—preaching, teaching, conversing, healing—only because He consistently claimed times to experience energy–restoring communication with God while alone. The serenity, stability, and security which Jesus demonstrated amid the chaotic swirl of the masses had its source in His regular periods of private prayer. What makes us think that we can do without what Jesus embraced as essential?

Beware of the idea that Jesus lived such a segmented life that He could only pray in private and minister in public according to an unalterable sequence. The Sea of Galilee provided Jesus a means of moving from public ministry to private prayer and back again. But more than once both ministry and prayer took place *on* the Sea of Galilee. Needs arose which caused Jesus to transform the place of transition into a place of action. So Jesus prayed as He made His way to a place of prayer. And He ministered as He journeyed to and from sites of ministry.

A PLACE OF FEAR AND FAITH

By far, the most memorable moments from Jesus' journeys on the Sea of Galilee involved storms. Is that not typical? Most people can more vividly recall the turbulent times of life— which explode like lightning flashes under dark, cloud–covered skies— than peaceful moments under a brilliant warm sun in a clear blue sky. Maybe pain and fear make more lasting impressions on us than do pleasure and peace. Or maybe we take the latter too much for granted.

High winds, loud claps of thunder, rough waters, and jagged bolts of lightning often characterize a place of transition. Moving from one town to another or from one relationship to another, losing a longtime career and having to retrain for a different kind of work, leaving home and beginning college, and launching an effort to turn a dream into reality involve tough transitions. So do grappling with doubt while seeking to develop a stronger faith, dealing with grief in an effort to get on with life after the death of a loved one, and trying to find another church when active membership in a home church is no longer possible. Transition and turbulence often seem synonymous.

Storms regularly swept across the Sea of Galilee, as they do in life itself, with blinding speed and fierce winds. Especially after mid–day. The gorges around the Sea of Galilee acted as wind tunnels through which cold air from the heights of Mount Hermon could rush down, crash into, and quickly displace the warm air hovering over the water. When that happened, a storm formed instantaneously and churned the water of the sea with incredible force. Anyone caught on the water when one of these blasts hit it—as Jesus was more than once—faced extreme danger.

Jesus was at His best in the face of storms—whether amid rolling waves of water on a lake, mounting anger among crowds gone wild in a city, or rapidly fluctuating emotions in an individual's life. Not one ever to turn His back on a bad situation, Jesus willfully entered storms in order to help the ones besieged by the storms. On the Sea of Galilee, the disciples of Jesus learned that if Jesus were not physically present with them when a storm arose, He would get to them as soon as possible—even if He had to walk.

Characteristically and compassionately Jesus addressed people's fears and invited faith. It was not just any kind of faith, though. It was not a naive, simplistic faith fascinated with positive thinking which flippantly confesses, "Don't worry. Everything is bound to be all right sooner or later." It was not an egotistical faith focused on the endless possibilities of self-potential. Ask Peter about that one. The man who joined Jesus on the choppy waters began thinking about himself, took his eyes off his master, and nearly drowned. Faith in God, faith in the Lordship of Christ—that is the kind of faith Jesus invited.

Knowing the fear which can dominate a place of transition, Jesus spoke to the storms—the one on the water and the one in the disciples—"Peace, be still" (Mark 4:39). And the storm subsided. The place of fear became a place of faith—because of Jesus.

At the Sea of Galilee in our souls, we learn how to confront fear and to acknowledge life's ultimate authority. In other words, we learn of the power of God to calm any kind of storm and to get us through the roughest of transitions. Thereby, we find the faith—God-oriented, Christ-centered faith—sufficient to sustain us in any situation.

A PLACE OF POTENTIAL

Travel to places of transition is never easy. Complications cloud decision-making. Pulls in opposite directions can stymie a person.

On the shore of the Sea of Galilee, Jesus longed for solitude. So He had the disciples prepare for a trip across water. But getting away was difficult. Crowds of people pulled at Jesus and pleaded for Him not to leave them. Jesus was tired, weary to the bone. He knew He would not be able to rest until He got away for a while. However, scores of individuals begged for healing. And so many people were desperate to learn about forgiveness. Such is the dilemma of a conscientious person on the verge of a major transition.

Had Jesus not moved away from the crowds periodically, however, He would have had nothing to offer them when He was with them. Periodic efforts to change the scenery in His life were good for Jesus—physically and spiritually.

Besides had Jesus not traveled back and forth across the Sea of Galilee, we might never have known the potential of a transition place and time in our lives, to say nothing of the power of Jesus to bring peace amid the storms which often accompany transitions. A transition place is not to be avoided or feared. No shame or disgrace is involved in going there. Everybody needs or has to make changes at one time or another.

Keep in mind, too, that moving across the Sea of Galilee, negotiating transition, is not mere relaxation. We may learn more of God's power during a period of transition than we would have ever known where we came from or discover where we are going. Christ is Lord of swirling winds and tumbling waves even as of blue skies and bright sunshine. Christ is Lord of the unemployed as well as of the employed, of folks bent by heavy burdens as well as of individuals who feel on top of the world, and of people who are bored to death with where they are as well as of individuals scared to death of where they are going. Christ is Lord of the places of transition in life even as of those places in which residence seems to be permanent or the sites which only exist in people's dreams.

People do well to familiarize themselves with the Sea of Galilee. A lot of folks will go there at their own initiative. Others, even those who want nothing to do with it, will find this place thrust upon them. Given the geography of a soul, sooner or later, everybody has to navigate a Sea of Galilee—no exceptions.

9

SAMARIA:
AN "OUT–OF–PLACE"
PLACE

He [Jesus] had to pass through Samaria.
— John 4:4

S AMARIA. SPEAK THE WORD with a scowl if you say
it at all. Only then will you begin to sense the antipa-
thy—no, the outright hatred—which most Jewish people felt toward the region of Samaria and the Samaritans
(spoken with lemony bitterness) who lived there. And Samaritans harbored similarly intense, equally negative feelings toward Jews. We cannot imagine the level of prejudice which
existed between the Jews and the Samaritans. Or, on second
thought, sadly, maybe we can understand.

No Jew wanted to go to or through Samaria, not even a mercenary–minded itinerant. It had nothing to do with the land, or ease of travel. The beauty of the hill country as well as the coastal plain and the Jordan Valley around it could be spectacular. And going through Samaria made the journey between Galilee and Judea easier, not more difficult.

People were the problem: "The people you have to put up with in Samaria!" Taking a less demanding route of travel by going through Samaria or enjoying the glories of the Samaritan countryside was not worth putting up with the people who lived there. "You don't want to go to Samaria. In fact, you'd better not go to Samaria."

Strange. Samaria does not seem all that far away or unfamiliar. It is not. For Jesus, Samaria was near to both Judea and Galilee. For us, Samaria can be as close as the other side of town or the back side of our hearts.

Almost any first century Jew knew that the Jordan Valley lay next to the eastern edge of Samaria as did the coastal plain to the west. In the north, the region of Samaria stopped at the Valley of Jezreel. An invisible line running from Jericho to the Valley of Ajalon defined the southern extremity of Samaria.

For us the dividing line between Samaria and everywhere else, Samaritans and everybody else, commonly consist of a set of railroad tracks, Main Street, the mills complex, or the "projects." Whether boundaries are visible or not, everybody understands where Samaria begins and ends. Residents on both sides of the divide often advise each other, "After sundown, I would not be caught dead over there."

Prejudice, though, knows no boundaries. Samaria is a rambling, spread–out place in the soul. The closer people get to Samaria, the less concern they have about kindness, sensitivity, and common courtesy. *What's the use?* they think, *Don't waste goodness on these good-for-nothings.*

After hearing firsthand Jesus' instructions about forgiveness and grace, His disciples wanted to call down fire on the Samaria of their day. Modern people choose other, more sophisticated methods of dealing with Samaria—methods not as overtly destructive, but every bit as harmful.

Financial officers "redline" the area known as Samaria (or "the West End," "the jungle," or "the slums") so that no one can move in or out of this district easily or secure funds for remodeling or new construction. Politicians rezone the Samarias in their domains to keep these areas tightly confined, thereby keeping Samaritans in their place. Entrepreneurs uproot long-term residents of a Samaritan community and leave them emotionally and geographically displaced under the guise of "cleaning up the neighborhood."

A PLACE OF ANTAGONISM

Jewish antagonism for Samaria stretched back for centuries. More than seven hundred years before the birth of Christ, Assyrians captured the northern kingdom of the Jewish people. As was the custom, the captors transported the captives out of their homeland and resettled them in Assyrian territory. At the same time, the captors replaced the exiled Jews with people from a variety of different places—Cutha, Ava, Hamath, Sepharvaim.

A few Jewish citizens of the Northern Kingdom escaped the Assyrian displacement and retained their homes. In subsequent years, these people intermarried with the new residents of the area. Racial purity vanished.

Years later, when the Southern Kingdom fell victim to the aggression of the Babylonians, a similar pattern was repeated, with one major exception. The captors transported Jewish residents of the south to Babylon. But these Jewish people remained unquestionably Jewish. They vigorously protected their racial purity.

Once their captivity ended, Jewish families from the south returned home and immediately began to rebuild the temple in Jerusalem. When the Samaritans—the Jewish people in the north who had intermarried with people of other races—heard about this development, some of them traveled to Jerusalem with an offer to assist in the revitalization of the temple. They met strong resistance. Their help was rejected. The racially pure Jews told the racially mixed Samaritans they had no right to work on the temple.

Bitterness developed between the Samaritans and the Jewish people, terrible bitterness. The Samaritans worshiped at a rival temple on Mount Gerizim, which a Jewish general finally destroyed. Samaritans studied their own edition of the Penta-teuch. Frequently, Jewish travelers in Samaria were roughed up, as were Samaritan travelers in Jewish territories.

When Jesus embarked on his ministry, the quarrel between the Jews and the Samaritans had existed for well over four hundred years. But the animosity between the two groups left the impression that one had perpetrated some violent atrocity on the other during the previous evening.

Most of us know better than we wish how long flames of anger, resentment, and prejudice can burn. The name of the place where it happens may be Samaria. Or, it may be Northern Ireland, Lebanon, or Bosnia. It may be a place in the heart, a spot in the soul where heated emotions never cool off.

Embittered people may come from the same family, live in the same state, or work for a common employer. Even after a period of relative calm, when their negative feelings do no more than smolder, one small disruption can ignite hot blazes of hatred which quickly leap out of control again.

Conscientious Jews refused to go through Samaria. Jesus did not, though.

A PLACE OF PREJUDICE

The region of Samaria rested between Galilee to the north and Judea to the south. This forty-mile-long, thirty–five-mile-wide block of high country dropped off sharply in the direction of the Jordan Valley.

Journeys between Judea and Galilee took approximately three days when a traveler took the route which ran through Samaria. However, those who wished to avoid Samaria had to cross the Jordan River prior to arriving in Samaria, travel up the eastern side of this body of water (going through Perea), and then, once beyond the region of Samaria, cross the Jordan again. This route took at least six days.

Time is of little consequence in the presence of great prejudice. So, most Jews did not mind going out of the way to avoid setting a foot on Samaritan soil, as if that would settle the matter. Of course, it did not. Jesus, however, refused to participate in such sickness. When He needed to move from Judea to Galilee as quickly as possible, Jesus set out through Samaria. Not only did He want to take this route, He felt compelled to take this route. My guess is that the urgent sense of direction behind Jesus' action had far more to do with demonstrating moral convictions than with saving travel time.

The Samaria in a soul, like its ancient counterpart in Palestine, separates people. For many individuals Samaria remains a navigational problem, not for movements of the body but for transitions of the spirit. Samaria stands in the way of people moving rapidly to where they need to be, traveling to where they ought to go.

Samaria is a place of prejudice—irrational, unjustifiable, reprehensible prejudice. At the Samaritan site in a person's spirit, individuals of different races receive condemnation because of their God-given identities. People from other cultures bear the brunt of vicious scorn as a result of being born in a distant part of the world. Even Christians who have a different worship style must shoulder harsh, critical judgments because their buildings and forms of worship are not identical with those of the prejudiced person.

Prejudice denies people the right to be who they are, as if an individual chose Samaritan parents knowing that Samaritans were at the lower end of the order of creation. Why, a Samaritan woman could no more alter having been born in Samaria than a Jewish male could change his entrance into the world through a Judean family committed to the priesthood. Prejudice rejects individuals because of conditions beyond their control.

Prejudice has social consequences as well. Prejudice blocks the potential for communication between people, shuts down opportunities for interaction, and destroys the possibility of building community.

Acting out of the Samaria in their souls, religiously–prejudiced individuals seek to wipe from the face of the earth individuals who hold faith convictions different from their own, individuals whom God has called them to love, not destroy. Politically–prejudiced people manipulate the power of government to institutionalize discrimination and segregation rather than facilitate reconciliation, Socially–prejudiced folks establish building codes to assure the cultural uniformity of certain neighborhoods. Economically–prejudiced people determine the value of a person by the numbers on the bottom line of that person's bank account, if he has one at all, and then treat that person accordingly.

The Samaria through which Jesus passed was a fertile, productive part of Palestine. Not so the Samaria of the soul. Nothing about this spot is productive. Absolutely nothing about this place attracts good feelings or contributes to helpful attitudes. The spiritual spot called Samaria is an ugly place.

Spiteful, hurtful myths run rampant there. Lies go with the territory. Prejudiced people perpetrate harmful labels and destructive stereotypes to justify their prejudice. You know the kind of trash–talk which goes on: "All Samaritans are lazy cheats. Turn your back on them and they will steal you blind." "Those money–grubbing Jews will never learn." "It's not safe in Samaria. You couldn't get me to go there to save my life."

At Samaria, we see life at its worst. Fear, resentment, anger, competition, and judgment fill the days of people who linger at this spiritual place. And the only promise to be found there, if you can call it a promise, is that unless prejudice is eradicated from Samaria, things will get worse.

A PLACE OF CHALLENGE

Samaria is a place which challenges faith. This site of prejudice seems so out–of–the–way, so different, that people wonder whether or not faith is relevant there: *Is Samaria off–limits to the normal expectations of faith, out of bounds for mercy, beyond the range of moral responsibility? Does Christianity, which works everywhere else in the world, find Samaria to be a place where it fails? Is faith inept when besieged by prejudice?*

Prejudice is an enemy of the faith proclaimed by Christ. To live by prejudice is to charge God with a major mistake, an error in divine judgment, a faux pas in creation. Prejudice allows people to be angry with God for not establishing their prejudices as the criteria by which all other people are judged.

A PLACE OF REALITY

Not only does the Samaria of the soul severely challenge faith, it dramatically tests the authenticity of love. In fact, Samaria is a place which exposes the reality of love or lack of it.

Often people who boast the loudest about their love for everybody else have the most difficulty demonstrating love in Samaria. Their actions tell the real story: *Love doesn't fit here. These people are different—not our kind; they will take advantage of loving actions. Surely God doesn't expect us to love such folks as these with the same kind of love we hold for people more like us.*

Several years ago, a black friend of mine spent a week as a guest preacher in an all-white church in a small town in the South. My friend and the host minister developed an exceptionally good relationship. All went well until one day after lunch when the two ministers returned to their car to find that someone had scrawled across its side with shoe polish: "Nigger lover." No sooner did he see the phrase splashed across his automobile than the host preacher flew into a rage, shouting, protesting, and stomping his feet. My black friend calmly called the pastor by name and encouraged him to be quiet. "All week long you have been telling me that you love me," he said to the distraught pastor. "Please don't get so upset because someone has written the truth on your car. It's nothing to be ashamed of."

Hatred and cruelty thrive in Samaria. Opportunities for prejudiced statements and discriminatory actions quickly cause a person to reveal whether he or she is living by real love or as an impostor emotion.

Jesus was fit for the challenge of Samaria—ready to demonstrate His faith in God there as elsewhere, ready to exhibit a love for Samaritans exactly like His love for all other people. So Jesus traveled to Samaria. He wanted to. And in many ways He felt He had to take this journey. In both His words and actions, Jesus broke long–established cultural traditions and disregarded the strict dictates of prejudice.

Ironic twists lurk in every shadow which falls across the landscape of Samaria. The Jewish people thought that by blasting Samaria verbally and avoiding it physically, they could be spared any dealings with this object of their prejudice. But that was not the case. It never is. Samaria and its residents became moral burrs pricking the consciences and scratching the spirits of the Jews, judging the ethical substance of their self–acclaimed righteousness, and questioning their devotion to the God who called for an indiscriminate, unconditional love for all people.

Samaria will not be denied attention. Prejudice cannot be ignored forever. All of us must face the conditions of this place at some point in our lives. At the Samaritan spot in our souls, we will either judge prejudice as evil and seek to get rid of it or accept prejudice as normal and find ourselves judged by it.

The "out–of–place" place, like the people who live there, can really disturb our travel plans. Getting ready for a visit to Samaria requires hard work—religious toil, moral labor. Sometimes I wish that, when the conversation between Jesus and

His disciples turned to travel through Samaria, Jesus had just left well enough alone. But He did not. And we cannot.

10

JERICHO: A PLACE OF SALVATION

He [Jesus] entered Jericho and was passing through.
— Luke 19:1

THE CITY OF JERICHO brings to mind many different words. But salvation is not one of them. Fear, yes. The road between Jerusalem and Jericho stretched across a terrifying desert. Intense heat killed all vegetation. Water was nowhere to be found. The rugged land was strewn with sharp stones and sliced apart by dangerous deep ravines and gaping gorges.

But that was not the worst of it. Robbers hid out in the limestone hills which surrounded the city of Jericho. These Bedouin thieves made a living sweeping down from these hills, attacking travelers, and making off with stolen goods. The notorious dangers of travel between Jerusalem and Jericho reached legendary proportions.

Beauty, certainly. Many people spoke of Jericho—which means "city of Palms," for a great palm forest gave the city early fame—as a new Eden or a little paradise. The contrast between the tropical fertility of the city and the arid wasteland of the desert could be breathtaking. Located by the Elisha–Spring, the people of Jericho had plenty of water to enrich the land. And what enrichment they did! Vast orchards of bananas, pomegranates, figs, and dates covered the city. The rose gardens of Jericho were known far and wide. Balsam groves were prolific, creating beauty for the eyes and filling the air with a wonderful scent of fine perfume. What a place. As cities go, Jericho was a thing of beauty.

Wealth. Affluent citizens had dotted Jericho with villas, parks, and pools—all symbols of their wealth. Visitors stood in awe of the abundance in this place. People traveled to Jericho to see the sights. It was widely known as a place of fun.

And commerce. Situated at an intersection of major caravan routes, Jericho benefited economically from a constant influx of itinerant businessmen. Heavy traffic filled the road which reached from Damascus to Arabia. Jericho's location in the Jordan Valley also allowed residents of the city to control the crossings of the river which gave people access to lands to the east. As exports like dates and balsam left Jericho, the coffers in Jericho grew fat. And tax–collectors experienced a bonanza. Jericho was a major taxation center in ancient Palestine.

Finally, politics. The warm climate of Jericho attracted the attention of Herod the Great, who built his winter capitol there—a magnificent marble palace. In time, Herod also constructed an impressive amphitheater and stout city walls. Archelaus added splendid gardens as well as other structures.

Jericho hosted political discussions from which came governmental decisions with far-reaching effects.

Talk of Jericho prompts thoughts of fear and fun, beauty and affluence, politics and commerce, taxes and robberies—but not salvation. To the contrary, Jericho represents the epitome of temptation; a place of so many activities and a promise of so much pleasure that people are tempted to view its offerings as viable substitutes for salvation, if thoughts of salvation ever enters their minds.

A PLACE OF EXTREMES

Risks accompany people on a trip to Jericho. However, these risks serve to heighten the thrill of the whole experience, not to deter it. Visitors to Jericho meet all kinds of people on the streets—the "up and out" who are admired and the "down and out" who are disparaged. A person could be accosted by a robber in the streets of Jericho or hassled by some kind of fanatic. At the same time, though, a tourist in the city might meet a famous publican, an impressive soldier, or a stately priest.

Curiosity seekers find fulfillment in Jericho. The variety and extremes of the personal situations encountered there enamor the inquisitive—a badly beaten man in a ditch, left for dead by a marauding band of robbers; a man up a tree for having exacted more taxes than the law allowed; an individual on top of the world, who is a picture of health, affluence, and success, and a beggar in desperate straits hobbling along looking for food.

People appear to get away with a lot of wrongdoing in Jericho. However, a careful look into the faces of several of these folks reveals a haunting hollowness and a disturbing expression of urgency to complete their search for something more.

We know Jericho. It is a city nearby or a place on the coast, perhaps even a tourist site across an ocean. Or maybe it is a spot in the heart dominated by relief from responsibilities, a vacation from spirituality, and freedom from moral principles. Spiritually, Jericho is the place we go for "time off" or to "do our own thing." At Jericho, no one seems to watch us. Even the few people who do take note of our behavior obviously do not care what they see. We know Jericho as a spiritual site in the geography of our souls, but not as a place of salvation.

At our own Jericho sometimes we feel that we are on top of the world and at other times we feel that the whole world is on top of us. In one day at Jericho, thrills shoot through our bodies as we enjoy a relationship as dangerous as it is desirable. But on another day, maybe even the very next day, sorrow saps our strength and depresses our spirits because the relationship with which we have flirted has soured. On one trip to Jericho we may count our money and decide we have everything we need, thinking that if we discover anything more we need and do not have, we can buy it. During a subsequent journey to Jericho, though, acknowledging that our hearts are as empty as our pockets and bank accounts, we admit that some things are not for sale.

A PLACE OF SALVATION

Jericho becomes a place of salvation when Jesus enters it—only then. Salvation is not for sale here, not even to the highest bidder. And salvation cannot be earned here, not even by the most radical over–achiever. Jericho becomes a place of salvation when amid the topsy–turvy activities of this place, among the haves and the have–nots, while some are achieving new heights of pleasure and others are bottoming out in pain, Jesus arrives.

What great, good news it is that Jesus enters Jericho. Jericho! Some people relegate Jesus entirely to holy places, denying that He would spend time with folks involved in a plethora of unholy pursuits. Others criticize Jesus for rubbing shoulders with sordid individuals, charging that He is running with the wrong crowd. A few individuals simply refuse to believe that Jesus would ever have anything to do with this kind of place, warning friends that if they go to Jericho they will never find Jesus. But they are wrong. Jesus travels to Jericho. And, when He does, Jericho becomes a place where people can discover salvation, whether in a person's soul or in the city not too far from Jerusalem.

For folks who know only the other side of Jericho's reputation—a refuge for debauchery, a city rocked by scandal, a place for riotous living, a spot which pushes the limits of decency––news that Jesus comes to Jericho is almost too good to be true. An announcement of Jesus' arrival sets off an explosion of soul–shaking thoughts: *A life near ruin can be rescued. Hurts––both those I caused by my foolishness and those I could not avoid––can be healed. My sins––the intentional ones which are so blatant and the more subtle ones which only a few other people know about––can be forgiven. This terrible guilt I carry because of my lack of integrity finally can be removed and a sense of wellbeing inserted in its place. Debts which I thought would follow me for the rest of my days can be repaid.* Remarkable! The place where my sins are most prominent in my vision is the very place where my sins can be forgiven!

Not many people travel to Jericho in search of salvation. But all who go to Jericho like all who live there need salvation. And all who need it can find it—not somewhere else but right here at Jericho.

Ask Zacchaeus. He was in the top of a tree, but in the pits of his life until he met Jesus. After an encounter with Jesus, everything in his life changed. Zacchaeus no longer needed to climb a tree to catch a vision of Christ or to hide in an obscure corner to escape the wrath of people around him. After Zacchaeus got his feet on the ground, with God's help, he began to get on top of his life—accepting the forgiveness offered by Jesus, righting old wrongs, paying overdue debts, and working at his job with both sensitivity and integrity.

Or ask the man with the scratched-up face, the badly beaten fellow whom a Samaritan traveler, taking a significant risk, had rescued from a ditch. A hated Samaritan helped this man when he was completely helpless.

As strange as it may seem, possibilities for salvation pervade the region in and around Jericho. Because Jesus is there and here.

Just when a woman has dabbled in everything that seems to have the most promise for life and found it all devoid of permanent meaning, salvation enters the picture as a potential which she can realize. As a man with depleted finances, scrambled emotions, and a broken spirit ponders putting an end to everything, he catches a vision of one who promises abundant life—even for a person like himself. Approaching Jericho, people who have tried to compensate for a lack of love in their lives by engaging in a variety of sexual liaisons find their depression over more and more relations producing less and less meaning confronted by Jesus' call to a covenant relationship.

A Place of Grace

Jericho is a place of grace, which is no surprise to anybody because salvation and grace always go together. Jesus offers people salvation as a result of grace.

Grace is better understood by images than by definitions: God's reaching out to offer forgiveness to people who have not even mouthed a word of repentance; Jesus' declaring love for a man who has rejected everything He has taught; a stranger's offering help to a troubled traveler and expecting nothing in return, not even a word of gratitude; a tax collector's returning stolen money, not dollar for dollar, but four dollars given for every one dollar taken. Grace rejects retaliation and works for reconciliation. Grace repays evil with good. Grace finds expression in actions which go far beyond fairness, equality, and justice. Grace has no interest in seeing people get what they deserve, only in a commitment to give people what they need.

Ironically, people who don't understand grace think that Jesus is as soft on sin as the pleasure peddlers who fill the streets of Jericho. "He just forgives sin and accepts sinners into the kingdom of God," they charge. "Why does He not exact some remorse from the sinners or inflict upon them a measure of punishment appropriate for their wrongdoings?" people want to know. "How can He love an unlovable person, accept a reprehensible wrongdoer, and offer salvation to both?"

Grace cannot be understood in the marketplace—any marketplace. Grace is not about bartering or buying and selling. A person of grace knows full well its cost but never asks a recipient to pay it. Grace ignores merit; its focus is always on the worth of love.

How can a place of sin become a place of grace and thus a site of salvation? They are one and the same when Jesus is there.

A man rushing into Jericho to get away from the responsibilities of his family and the dictates of his conscience can run headlong into Jesus. Suddenly the place he has so feverishly sought as a place of sin becomes the spot where he receives salvation.

You cannot always tell a grace place by outward appearances. The site of great grace can be a faraway city or a familiar household, a sophisticated night spot or a sleazy dive, a mansion or a shanty. Since grace goes everywhere, salvation can happen anywhere.

The Jericho of a person's heart is no different. An occasion of sin becomes an opportunity for grace. Life–giving hope emerges in a context of crippling despair. At the moment when we feel we are at our wits' end, a possibility arises for the salvation of our souls to begin.

Jericho is a place to which everybody goes, at least spiritually. It can look for all the world like an inviting carnival of fun through disobedience, or it can appear as a frightening hellhole. Whichever the place is, nobody can find lasting satisfaction there.

Jericho is a place to which Jesus travels. And once He is there, everything can change. People in Jericho can ignore Jesus and give themselves to serious sinning, or hurting sinners looking for relief by way of more sin can bump into Jesus. Once Jesus arrives in Jericho, this place in the heart becomes the site where the greatest need in life can be met immediately.

Even if we set out for Jericho for a reason unrelated to salvation, we may end up thanking God that amid the futility of our own pursuits we run straight into the divine Presence who gives abundant life. Salvation may not be the first thought which comes to our minds when we think of Jericho—but it can be the last.

11

CAESAREA PHILIPPI: A PLACE OF CLARIFICATION

. . . Jesus came into the district of Caesarea Philippi . . .
— Matthew 16:13

W HEN A PERSON HAS to get away, to pull back, to find a place to be quiet and sort things out, Caesarea Philippi offers everything that person needs. Caesarea Philippi is a place of beauty where one can sit quietly and reflect on God's goodness in creation or ponder the peace of God which can bring inner calm amid a harried situation. At Caesarea Philippi, an individual can find relief from the demands of other people hawking their own agenda. While enjoying the region of Caesarea Philippi, a person can get an honest perspective on life, clarify priorities, acknowledge the challenges immediately ahead, experience renewal, and hear the voice of God.

Anyone who does not have a Caesarea Philippi to go to when life needs to be slowed down must find such a place within the soul. Life gets out of kilter without a visit to this place. At Caesarea Philippi—the internal one or an external spot—a person can relax and enjoy beauty or engage in the kind of serious conversation and reflection which yield a life-enhancing clarification of reality.

At a critical point in His ministry, Jesus took His disciples and withdrew to the extremity of Caesarea Philippi for a period of retreat. Given the inviting reputation of this region and the exhausting drain of interaction with the crowds, the disciples must have rejoiced when they learned their destination. Caesarea Philippi was far removed from Galilee, Judea, the temple, synagogues, scribes, and Pharisees.

Comfortably situated along one of the angular terraces of Mount Hermon which was surrounded by three opulently fertile valleys, Caesarea Philippi offered a profusion of greenery—vines, mulberry and fig trees, and a wide variety of other types of vegetation. Interspersed with the greenery were breath-taking protrusions of rock, some jutting into view high above the ground and others sweeping downward in sheer cliffs that looked like carefully planned walls.

Caesarea Philippi stood at the head waters of the Hermon River. A sensitive listener in this place could hear rushing water produced by the snows of Mount Hermon beginning its one hundred mile journey to the Dead Sea. Water from the Jordan River plunged out of a cave in one of the one-hundred-and-fifty-foot-high cliffs.

Visitors to Caesarea Philippi could spend all their time gazing at the scenery, admiring the beauty, reveling in the wonder of nature's gifts. Not Jesus, though. Jesus brought His disciples to Caesarea Philippi for a specific purpose. He needed to know what these men were thinking and feeling about Him and His ministry. He wanted to find out what other people were saying as well.

Some people avoid confronting reality. "What you don't know can't hurt you," they say. Such folks thrive on denial, if not ignorance. A dose of reality is like bad medicine for them. These people do not want to know what other folks think, what challenges lie ahead, how life is going.

Harboring troublesome thoughts, Jesus traveled with His disciples to Caesarea Philippi to measure reality: *Is my ministry being understood? Are the twelve disciples growing in their knowledge of God and the purposes of God? How do they see Me? Are they prepared for what lies ahead? Do they see Me as the Messiah? If so, what kind?*

A PLACE OF INTERROGATION

Caesarea Philippi was a place of interrogation. Jesus asked His disciples what people were saying about Him, "Who do men say that the Son of man is?" (Matt. 16:13). After listening to their answers—"Some say John the Baptist; and others, Elijah; but still others, Jeremiah, or one of the prophets" (Matt. 16:14)—Jesus pressed harder. He asked the disciples, "But who do you say that I am?" (Matt. 16:15).

Jesus chose a place for raising these questions. Caesarea Philippi had long been associated with the worship of a wide variety of deities. Ruins of a temple which Herod the Great constructed in 20 B.C. could be seen clearly. Statues of idols stood in the crevices of the massive cliffs towering over this group of men. Three shrines had been carved into the wall–like slab of stone. The cave from which the waters of the Jordan came rushing had previously served as a heathen sanctuary for worshipers of the god Pan. In fact, an inscription carved into the rocky wall over this cavern read, "Priest of Pan" (or "Pan and the Nymphs" as another translation suggests).

We understand this place called Caesarea Philippi. Most of us have been there spiritually if not physically. Times come when we confront people with different religious loyalties. As friends display the symbols of their commitment to a deity called success, we wonder about a faith which defines success in terms of service. As we watch the triumph of those who worship the gods of power, we ask ourselves about the wisdom of serving a savior who praised weakness.

At Caesarea Philippi difficult questions demand honest answers: *Do I really believe in God? If so, what kind of God do I believe in? Is my faith shaped more by what I have come to know about God personally or by what I hear other people say? What is the nature of my relationship with Christ? No pretending, no cliches, no second–hand comments—by my actions as well as my words, what do I reveal about the authority of Christ in my life?*

People who refuse to confront important questions about themselves never come to an honest understanding of themselves. A part of the dubious genius of personhood is an ability to put up a front by which we can fool ourselves as well as others. But God is not fooled. And we need to know about ourselves what God knows about us. Caesarea Philippi is an important place in our souls—the place where we confront and answer fundamental questions about ourselves and our faith.

A PLACE OF REVELATION

Amid Jesus' questions about His identity, Simon Peter blurted out, "You are the Christ, the Son of the living God" (Matt. 16:16). Like the hush which follows a blinding flash of lightning or a booming clap of thunder, silence followed Peter's statement. Only Jesus could respond. What Jesus said to Simon Peter—"flesh and blood has not revealed this to you, but My Father who is in heaven" (Matt. 16:17)—left no doubt that Caesarea Philippi was *a place of revelation*. Peter answered Jesus' question correctly, but his accuracy was not because of his brilliance. Peter served as a medium of divine revelation. God spoke through this rugged fisherman.

The most helpful guidance in dealing with life's greatest dilemmas comes not from personal opinion but from divine revelation. Personal judgments are important, but nowhere near as important as insights into the wisdom and will of God. At Caesarea Philippi comments which begin with "I think" or "in my opinion" must ultimately give way to a reception of truths provided by God.

What is most important at Caesarea Philippi is not what we or others think, but what God reveals. The cultural indoctrination which people bring to this spiritual site often makes a stay here difficult. That truth resounds throughout the region of Caesarea Philippi: Perception is not reality; reality is reality.

Popular perceptions of Jesus identified Him as John the Baptist, Elijah, or Jeremiah. Virtually everyone was talking about Jesus as a prophet. Had a popular vote been taken, Jesus would have no doubt been identified as a former prophet who had come back to life. That was a consensus opinion—but it was wrong!

Perception is not reality. People who build their lives upon popular opinions risk a reliance upon foundations which crumble under the weight of truth. Image builders, show makers, advertising moguls, and propagandists can affect the mentality and priorities which we bring to Caesarea Philippi. But to allow the work of these opinion shapers to determine what we take away from this spiritual spot is to waste whatever amount of our time we spend there. We might as well have been watching television as talking to Christ.

Caesarea Philippi is a place for confronting reality—not as colored by popular perceptions but as defined by revelations from God. This confrontation well may lead to more questions: *Do I accept Jesus as the Christ? Is my way of life shaped more by the Word of God or by the opinions of my peers? When I make important decisions, do I pay more attention to cultural mores or to biblical truths?*

Reality can make us very uncomfortable, but knowing the truth cannot harm us. God calls us to live out real faith in the real world. Such a life either begins at the Caesarea Philippi place in the soul or finds there the encouragement to continue.

A PLACE OF CLEAR ANSWERS

The questions, conversations, confessions, and revelation which form the substance of the spiritual Caesarea Philippi in our lives combine to give this place its most definitive identity. Caesarea Philippi is a place of clarification.

Surrounded by the grandeur of babbling waters, towering cliffs, and a riot of greenery, Jesus clarified several important matters: who people thought He was, how His own disciples identified Him, and the truth of God's revelation about Him. Of course, the disciples of Jesus shared in and benefited from this experience. Even then, however, their old, incorrect ideas did not die easy deaths.

After a clarification of His identity, Jesus moved quickly to clarify the nature of His ministry. For the first time, Jesus spoke with certainty about the inevitability of suffering in His future. The same disciple who had declared, "You are the Christ!" with equal vigor protested, "God forbid it, Lord!" (Matt. 16:22) Not even a medium of God's revelation could resist the temptation to assume he knew more than Christ did. Peter was not unique.

Individuals often confuse religion—even Christianity—with looking into a mirror, seeing their own faces, observing their own lifestyles, and concluding that they have seen God and discovered God's will. Personal wishes get mixed up with the divine will. Individual aspirations take on the nature of holy goals. Taking for granted that what God wants for their lives coincides with what they want for themselves, such people practice a faith oriented toward acceptance, success, and ease. Exuberance and commitment come easily.

Without a visit to Caesarea Philippi our assumptions about following Jesus may never be challenged—or corrected, if they are wrong. The disciples had never imagined that the Messiah would have to suffer. Death was completely out of the question. And these were not merely personal opinions. For generations, Jewish traditionalists and outstanding religious leaders alike had taught that the Messiah of God would rule with power. No one ever mentioned suffering.

Caesarea Philippi was a place of clarification. Jesus clearly identified any person who attempted to dissuade Him from following a path which involved suffering as an instrument of evil, a hindrance to the gospel.

We may become uneasy at Caesarea Philippi wondering which of our assumptions about Christianity are false. *Does following Jesus not mean experiencing success in family life, business enterprises, and social involvements? Does Jesus expect more from me than occasional confessions of His lordship? Am I confusing God's commission with my own personal ambitions? Surely, suffering is no longer a component of Christian discipleship—or is it? Am I at all like Simon Peter, a confessor of Christ who suddenly has turned into a hindrance to Christ's work?*

Everybody has to have answers—to know the correct answers—to these questions. Caesarea Philippi is the spot in our souls where that can happen. At this strategic site along our spiritual landscape, revelation from God addresses the most pressing questions of our lives. The result is clarification—clarification about who we are, who Jesus is, the nature of the Christian life, what we should be doing, and where we ought next to be going.

Needless to say, this place of clarification is not always a place of beauty, but it is an essential, indispensable stop on a healthy spiritual journey. As a matter of fact, without spending time at the clarification place, people can chase after false saviors and expend themselves in activities which have nothing to do with serving Christ. Worse still, without the clarity which comes from Caesarea Philippi, individuals can get themselves crucified on needless crosses which cause meaningless deaths.

12

MOUNT HERMON: A PLACE OF MYSTERY

. . . He [Jesus] went up to the mountain . . .
— Luke 9:28

I N THE JEWISH MIND, A MOUNTAIN represented closeness to God in much the same manner as a sea represented distance from God. Little wonder, then, that mountains occupied places of prominence and importance throughout the ministry of Jesus—the call of His disciples, His great message on the meaning of citizenship in the kingdom of God, a commission sending His followers into a world–wide mission, and, of course, the Transfiguration. On numerous other, lesser–known occasions, Jesus traveled to hilly or mountainous regions.

In beautiful, mystical language, the psalmist wrote, "I lift my eyes to the mountains; from whence shall my help come?

My help comes from the Lord" (Ps. 121:1–2). Such was the spirit in which Jesus climbed mountains and invited His disciples to do the same.

But what does this mean for people who live on ground which is so flat that not even a small mound of earth is visible to the naked eye? Where will they get their help? Does God favor high places so much that people who dwell in low places are in trouble when it comes to divine assistance?

In Jesus' ministry "mountaintop experiences" for the soul did not always require being on a mountaintop. In fact, not all New Testament narratives associate Jesus' call of the disciples with a mountain. In Luke's Gospel, the teaching usually referred to as "the Sermon on the Mount" takes place on a plain.

Lofty peaks of spiritual grandeur can be experienced by people physically at or below sea level. Take Mount Hermon, for example, the Mount Hermon in the soul.

Only six days after departing from Caesarea Philippi, Jesus, along with three of His disciples, ascended Mount Hermon—a peak which rose 9,000 feet above sea level and towered 11,000 feet above the Jordan Valley. The journey between the two places was not a long one, only about fourteen miles, but it was an important one.

Spiritually as well as physically, a close kinship exists between Caesarea Philippi and Mount Hermon. Typically, when things go right at Caesarea Philippi, a person is extremely eager to get on to Mount Hermon. Most spiritual pilgrims find both locales to be essential stopping places on their journey. But neither is like the other—and Mount Hermon is like nothing else in the world.

Jesus traveled to Mount Hermon needing a word from God. Immediately behind Him was an extended conversation at

Caesarea Philippi generally clarifying the public's perceptions of His identity and specifically exposing His disciples' thoughts regarding Him and His ministry. After mixed responses from the public Jesus wanted confirmation from God that He was following the right course of action. The opinions of the masses and the sentiments of one's closest friends are important, but no person's confession rivals in importance a declaration from God.

Success in Jesus' ministry had begun to cause major problems. With every victory came controversy. A showdown was on the near horizon. Jesus had no intention of attempting to dodge any difficulty; however, He did want to be sure He was pleasing God. Jesus climbed Mount Hermon seeking assurance.

A PLACE OF HOLINESS

Mount Hermon is a place where visitors sense they should take off their shoes. Its holy ground. What happened atop this mountain can be described but not explained. Mystery—rich, thick mystery—hovers over the entire experience called the Transfiguration like the cloud which covered the mountaintop while Jesus prayed.

While Jesus was praying at the summit of Mount Hermon, something happened to His appearance. Suddenly, Jesus looked as if He were no longer of this earth. His appearance radiated glory—whatever that means. Jesus glowed.

Then, Elijah and Moses appeared on the mountain and began conversing with Jesus. Certainly that was an other–worldly—or at least a different–world–based—happening. Here were the chief steward of the law and the prototype of all the prophets expressing affirmation and demonstrating support of Jesus' ministry.

As if all of that were not enough, a cloud appeared over the mountain—a cloud reminiscent of the one so often mentioned in the Old Testament as a representation of the *shekinah* glory of God. God was on the mountain. And the voice which came from the cloud gave every indication of being the voice of God. "This is my beloved Son, listen to Him," the voice—God—said. No sooner had silence settled across the mountaintop again than the four men who heard the voice realized that the same voice had spoken virtually the same words three years earlier at the Jordan River.

Mark's gospel account of this experience states that Peter, James, and John—the disciples whom Jesus had taken up the mountain with Him—were "exceedingly afraid" (Mark 9:6). Who would not have been scared to death? Surely Mark penned this understatement flashing a compassionate smile. Briefly stated, that is what happened on Mount Hermon.

Most people probably see Mount Hermon as one spot visited by Jesus which is completely without parallel in the spiritual experience of any other individual. What person can speak of an appearance transformed to radiate glory, of a conversation with religious leaders who died ages ago, of seeing a cloud which looks like the tabernacling presence of God, and of hearing a voice which sounds like the voice of God? Nowhere along the soulscape of our lives do we find a site which seems to be even remotely similar to Mount Hermon.

But in every soul, a place of mystery can be found. Great thinkers go so far as to say that mystery is a person's truest home. Certainly mystery stands at the center of authentic faith. And mystery abounds with meaning—the most profound meaning of life. There is the mountain. The place of mystery in a person's experience is the Mount Hermon in that person's soul.

Analysis and explanations are not worth much on Mount Hermon. Mystery cannot be analytically explained and remain mystery. That's the whole point of mystery. Only observations help. Mystery can be observed. And out of reverent observation can come statements of relevant meaning.

Jesus' experience at the summit of Mount Hermon defies interpretation, but it welcomes—indeed invites—observation. Kneeling or standing barefoot at Mount Hermon, those of us who ponder the meaning of what happened there among Jesus and three of His disciples begin to see the crucial importance of this peak clearly visible in the geography of our souls.

A PLACE OF VISION

Mount Hermon is a place of vision. It is an intersection between two worlds—the physical world and the spiritual world. Though those two words "spiritual" and "world" really do not belong together, I know of no other way to write about the other world, the world normally not seen but every bit as real as anything seen. So goes mystery.

A visionary is a person who stands in one world and peers into another world. A vision is an experience in which an individual sees more than other people can notice, despite how hard they look. Another part of reality appears via a vision, perhaps a part of reality which most of the time is not considered reality at all. When a vision occurs, one realm of life intersects another realm of life. Beneficiaries of a vision can never again look at life the same way they did before the vision occurred.

123

Visions deliver us from thinking that all there is to life is what we can see from where we sit or stand. How we do need an exodus from that kind of thought!

Surely there is more to justice than we see on the streets of our cities and in the courts of our nation. Undoubtedly peacemaking is more important than it appears in a society which frequently labels an advocate for peace as myopic or chicken. Life has to have more meaning than rolling out of bed at the sound of an alarm clock every morning, working through the hassle of daily routines, and wearily falling to sleep while watching the evening news on television. Yes, yes! People with a vision see God's justice which is absolute, God's blessing for peacemakers, and God's presence which transforms the realm of the ordinary into a holy arena inviting worship.

Entertaining a vision is like throwing open the shutters and raising the window on a cloudless day. Sunlight floods into a room which has been locked in uninterrupted darkness so long that the air is cold, damp, and stale. Having a vision is like traveling to Switzerland for the first time, arriving there after dark, and the first thing the next morning looking out a window and being awe struck by the snow–capped Swiss Alps. Mount Hermon is such a good place.

Visions lift our spirits, broaden our perspectives, and renew our strength. Visions save us. We understand why the Old Testament writer observed that without a vision, people perish (see Prov. 29:18).

With the help of a vision, a person can stand beside a loved one in the recovery room of a hospital, ponder the news of a positive biopsy, and know that life is bigger than this one moment. With vision, a young person discouraged by low test scores which may keep her out of the profession she wanted to pursue realizes that her future is more than numbers on a quiz.

A homeless man, a displaced elderly woman, an unmarried pregnant teenager, a businessman rocked by scandal, a couple unfairly accused of wrongdoing, a church locked into a program of weekly routines, and a person of faith who has become bored by faith—all of these can be saved by a vision.

And not all visions come on mountaintops. Thank God. People can experience visions when they travel to the Mount Hermon spot in their souls. What Jesus learned on a distant mountain in northeastern Palestine in the first century, we can learn along the close–as–our–hearts spiritual terrain of our lives—now.

Spend time at the Mount Hermon site in the geography of your soul. There you will see that life is more than it appears. You will know that God is active in our world—leading people willing to be led. You will realize an abundance of justifications for faith, incentives to love, reasons for hope.

The kind of vision which enabled Jesus to proceed to Jerusalem knowing full well that trip would end in crucifixion may be an incentive for us to get up in the morning when we would much prefer to put a pillow over our head and stay in bed; a motivation to expend our energies in a cause every bit as controversial as it is right; a reason for setting aside regular times to worship God and to be involved in the life of a community of faith when innumerable peers sneeringly label the practice of faith as worthless.

When people pray intently, keep their eyes wide open, and listen sensitively, they discern unusual, maybe even mystical, sights and sounds. Visions come. Where that happens is the Mount Hermon of the soul. It is a place of mystery.

A PLACE OF REVELATION

Mount Hermon is also a place of revelation. On that distant peak, God spoke. And every time God speaks, revelation happens. Subsequently, people—recipients of the divine disclosure; all the people who hear or see—know something about the nature of God, the reality of life, and the will of God within life not known before.

Revelation—a revelation from God—unfolded underneath, above, in, and through the mystical events which transpired on Mount Hermon. Once the vision faded, the cloud evaporated, and the voice was silenced, Jesus knew that God approved of Him and His ministry. And the three disciples also knew for sure, if previously they had hosted any doubts, that Jesus was indeed the Son of God.

When Joan of Arc stood before King Charles VII of France to explain her involvement in the French army's resistance to invading English soldiers, she spoke of voices. The eighteen-year-old peasant lady told the king about feeling God's presence and hearing God's voice calling her to action. Exasperated because this young woman could hear voices which he could not hear, King Charles VII shouted at Joan, "O your voices, your voices! Why don't the voices come to me? I am the King of France, not you!"[1]

Calmly Joan of Arc explained to the king that voices did come to him—the same voices which addressed her—but he could not hear them because he failed to really listen and pray. "They [the voices] do come to you," Joan told the sovereign, "but you do not hear them. You have not sat in the field in the evening listening for them. . . but if you prayed from your heart, and listened to the thrilling of the bells in the air after they stop ringing, you would hear the voices as well as I do."

At the Mount Hermon location in the soul, a young woman ready to drop out of medical school hears a voice telling her to continue; a man at the end of his wits over a bad marriage finds the inspiration to stay with his wife of five years and keep working on their relationship; a high school senior experiences a call to ministry; an elderly woman who often wonders why she has been left alone in the world sees that God has a purpose for her life. Mount Hermon is a place of revelation about callings and vocations, individual goals and marital relationships, life purposes and social involvements. Revelation comes to the mountain and to those who are there receive the revelation with joy. God speaks to people who pray at Mount Hermon.

In the ministry of Jesus, a trip to a mountain resulted in a time of prayer. During their visits to the heights with Jesus, His disciples realized that learning about God on the summit of a mountain and serving God by helping troubled people in a valley are one continuous act. On the top of first one mountain and then another, Jesus benefited from a vision and found direction through God's revelation. No wonder Jesus sought out a mountain and climbed it regularly.

Mystery? Yes, of course, especially on mountains like the one known as Hermon. But it is not a fear–inducing mystery; it is an inviting mystery. On the mountains in our souls we come face to face with a welcome mystery which instills security and inspires hope, which fills life with meaning and purpose.

Jesus ascended many mountains, Mount Hermon in particular. So do we. Whether we take an actual step upward is really irrelevant.

PART III

A Place of Passion and Death

13

JERUSALEM: A PLACE OF FICKLE FAITH

> . . . Jesus was coming to Jerusalem.
> — John 12:12

ON THE SUNDAY PRIOR TO His death, Jesus entered the city of Jerusalem riding on a donkey. Disciples traveled with Him. Onlookers shouted greetings and praises. Children laughed and played. Civil officials worried about order. Priests plotted strategies to capture Him.

Jerusalem. The word itself means "place of peace," literally "foundation of Shalom." How ironic. The city never had been peaceful. Conflict was constant between Jewish residents and Roman occupants in Jerusalem; between Jewish nationalists and loyalists to the foreign–based government. A war of words and ideas often escalated into episodes of deadly violence.

Not even religionists were free of turmoil in Jerusalem. Various factions of the religious community defined ortho-doxy differently. Sound doctrine could be defended by a knife–wielding attack on one's foes as well as by vigorous theological debates.

A quick scan of the Jerusalem landscape was telling. Walls were everywhere—walls for protection, walls for segregation. An old wall containing sixty towers surrounded the city it-self,buttressed by a newer wall with fourteen towers. One wall stood in the middle of the city—a residue of the military strategy of Jonathan Maccabee. Walls enclosed the numerous fortresses which had been constructed within the city. Even Jewish worship in Jerusalem took place behind walls. Jerusalem was a city of walls, not a place of peace.

Still, people greatly admired the city. It was a place of beauty. Wealthy residents had built impressive palaces there. A six-thousand-square-foot mansion overlooked the temple area. Many ancient monuments in Jerusalem reflected architectural genius. Hezekiah's huge, incredible tunnel—cut through 1750 feet of solid rock—carried water from the Virgin's Fountain to the residents. Caesar's theater and amphitheater adorned the city. An immense, eye–catching bridge spanned the "Valley of the Cheesemongers," connecting the eastern and western hills of Jerusalem. Buildings associated with government and relig-ion stood out prominently all over the city. And at night, the illumination of the magnificent temple compound was breath-taking.

In addition to its attractiveness, Jerusalem was a place of glory economically. Government offices held affluent treasur-ies. Major trade routes intersected in Jerusalem. Commerce thrived. No less than seven specialty markets complemented the expansive upper and lower markets where people traded vegetables, animals, and other goods. Shops and bazaars lined Jerusalem's narrow side streets. Some trades made use of the main thoroughfares of the city. Shoppers in Jerusalem could purchase all of the normal staples of a household plus well over one hundred imported articles.

More than anything else, though, Jerusalem was a holy place; indeed, the epitome of religious sites. The silver trumpets of the priests awakened the inhabitants of Jerusalem with their call to prayer each day. Music from the Levites could be heard throughout the area.

The temple dominated the city—literally and figuratively, physically and spiritually. Smoke from innumerable sacrifices sometimes hung in the air as a cloud. Thousands of pious people longing to visit the temple on one sort of religious pilgrimage or another filled the streets of the city. Additionally, hundreds of synagogues were open to the nearly quarter of a million people who lived in Jerusalem.

Jerusalem was a city of faith. But what kind of faith? Why did this "holy city" often seem so unholy? Immediately prior to entering Jerusalem at the end of His public ministry, why did Jesus weep after looking at the city?

Answers to these questions began to emerge when Jesus entered Jerusalem that Sunday, now known in tradition as "Palm Sunday." People unfamiliar with these answers had best pay careful attention to them and learn from them because Jerusalem is a spiritual spot in the soul of every person every bit as much as it was a religious shrine in first century Palestine.

Most everyone encounters Jerusalem at one time or another. Jerusalem is the mixed–up spot in the soul—a place of fickle faith, a center for confused convictions, a place of extreme vacillation where spontaneously Jesus is offered a heartfelt welcome and then suddenly driven away.

What happened in Jerusalem? What happens in the soul? How can faith appear so authentic and so hypocritical at the same time? We need to know. Just as certainly as Jesus sought entry into Jerusalem in the past, Jesus seeks entry into every person's life in the present. What happened in Jerusalem? What kind of place is Jerusalem?

A PLACE OF TRADITION

Jerusalem is a place which prefers tradition to revelation. No sooner had Jesus entered Jerusalem than tradition viciously lashed out at Him. Before He left, it clobbered Him.

Appearances can be so deceptive. The pervasive presence of religion in Jerusalem mightily impressed visitors to the city. Longtime residents of Jerusalem could be heard boasting that their religion had not changed in hundreds of years. Folks did what their ancestors had done. Priests said what their predecessors had said. Everybody knew the dominant religious traditions so well that rituals of worship could be performed blindfolded—and mindlessly.

In Jerusalem, the past provided an answer to every significant question regarding faith. No one wanted any new answers. And any thought of a need for new questions was considered ridiculous.

People in Jerusalem loved God's Word. Scholars carefully studied ancient sacred writings. Almost everyone spoke intelligently about what happened to Moses, how Amos preached, and the substance of Isaiah's vision. However, people failed to apply to the situations around them the truths which they gleaned from scriptural interpretations. The possibility that

God could speak to them in the present never even occurred to many people. Tragically, people who could clearly discern the divine voice in the lives of their ancestors did not even recognize God's efforts to address their own lives.

A blind loyalty to tradition produces religious people who are forever looking back over their shoulders in order to see where they should be going. A morally upright individual becomes a person unusually uptight about religion. Doing right is equated with doing what has always been done. Faithfulness to the divine will is defined in terms of conformity to a static precedent rather than as commitment to the dynamic God. It happened in Jerusalem. It happens in the Jerusalem of our souls.

Jesus did not conform to all of Jerusalem's popular traditions. He spoke as no previous religious leader had ever spoken. Jesus exuded an authority which was without precedent or parallel. Jesus demanded a decision about God's in-breaking reign. He offered forgiveness and invited conversion. Jesus commended an ethic based not on the letter of the law but on the leadership of God's spirit.

To say that the people in Jerusalem were uncomfortable with Jesus is an understatement. The more important religious tradition was to a person, the more Jesus disturbed that person. Many people agreed that they had enough of Jesus: *Even if He means well, Jesus breaks precedents and alters sacred traditions. We can't allow this to happen. We have to have something to hold on to. Everybody does. The practices of our ancestors were good enough for them. Surely they are good enough for us as well.*

With a unique opportunity to meet God face to face, to hear the Word of God with their own ears, and to see the work of God with their own eyes, scores of people in Jerusalem turned on Jesus. They preferred the comfortable security of a familiar religious tradition to the potentially disruptive challenge of a radically new revelation from God.

Faith was fickle in Jerusalem. But I am not casting stones. Jerusalem is an all too familiar stopping place in my own spiritual pilgrimage, a prominent, almost unmistakable point in the makeup of my soul. And I doubt if I am unique.

Living with what God said yesterday is easier than seeking to discern what God is saying today. Routinely doing everything as it has always been done provides protection from the discomfort of making changes and absolution from the worry of even thinking about new possibilities.

Risks—terrific risks—accompany such a situation. Participation in religious activities can become the products of thoughtless instincts rather than of true devotion. Routines can replace commitments. Change becomes a sin. Innovation is considered blasphemy. New ideas are rejected as heresy. Traditions about God are preferable to revelations from God.

Jerusalem is well known; it is familiar territory.

A PLACE OF FORM

Tradition is not the only serious problem in Jerusalem, though. Every bit as important is the fact that Jerusalem is a place where religious form is made a substitute for spiritual substance.

Religious practices abounded in the Jerusalem of Jesus' passion. People placarded scripture verses on the doorposts of their dwelling places. Priests walked around the city in sacred garbs. Occasionally, people stopped in the middle of the crowded market and prayed aloud. For the most part, the religious rituals so integral to life in Jerusalem were impressive and inspiring—and empty.

Fidelity to the forms of religious actions had replaced the substance of religious devotion. Most people spoke all of the conventionally "right" words and performed all of the carefully prescribed ritual acts. But the doing and the speaking had become ends in themselves. Offering the sacrifice of a bird without blemish in the temple had replaced seeking to serve God faithfully with a pure heart. Talk about love sufficed for concrete expressions of love.

Revealed religion was in real trouble in Jerusalem. Proper appearances had become more important than nurturing authentic faith. What an outrage would have resulted if a priest had worn vestments of the wrong color on a festival day. How disgraceful it was considered when a worshiper botched the recitation of a well–known psalm. But what of sincere worship pervaded by true praise for God? Was anyone concerned about that?

Nowhere in Jerusalem was the problem of form substituted for substance more obvious than in the temple. Busyness abounded. Faith was scarce. This place of worship preserved its promise as a house of worship for all people. But if a Gentile even attempted to pray there—no way would he be allowed to do so.

At first glance, all the people scurrying around in the temple seemed intent on making meticulous preparations to assure the acceptability of their offerings to God. It certainly was impressive. A closer look, however, showed a massive manipulation of religious motives for personal gain—a gross materialistic gouging of innocent people rather than exemplary service to God. And that was disgusting!

Preoccupation with the forms of religion made the practice of real religion almost impossible. Careful attention to tools for strengthening faith took the place of a concern for faith.

Rituals intended to aid religious education and inspiration became the objects of idolatrous adoration.

Ironically, at the same time people were plotting strategies to get rid of Jesus, they continued their holy rituals as usual—at the same time, in the same place, many of the same people. So empty was faith and so full was an interest in the forms of faith in Jerusalem that individuals ostensibly committed to righteousness planned to execute the Son of God in the Name of God!

How well we know Jerusalem. All too familiar in the soul is that place where form is confused with substance. Jerusalem is the birthplace of that driving desire to look holy even when possessing no more than a negligible interest in being holy. Style supplants content. *How* to speak words and sing hymns is more important than *what* is communicated through speaking and singing.

Jerusalem is that spiritual site where we pay more attention to the proper posture and grammar of prayer than to the nature of prayer itself. At this place, a specific type of worship holds priority over worship. Going to church is more significant than what takes place in church. Giving a tithe financially suffices for offering God every dimension of one's life.

The practice of religion is not too difficult in Jerusalem. Keeping the rituals of faith is always easier than embracing the substance of faith. Looking good wins hands down over struggling to be good. As long as spoken words acclaim love, the heart can harbor hatred. Parroting pious platitudes excuses spreading vicious rumors. Studying the texts of the Bible lessens the importance of living by biblical truths.

Peers can be impressed by appearances rather easily. But what about God? The God revealed in the Bible is interested in the actual substance of personal faith, not in traditional forms by which a person suggests faith to the public, whether or not it is really a fact of life.

In the course of my spiritual pilgrimage, I have spent far too much time in Jerusalem. This spot is well known in my soul.

A PLACE OF ENTHUSIASM

Jerusalem is a place where enthusiasm suffices for commitment. In fact, in Jerusalem people often mistake sheer excitement for righteousness.

No dearth of enthusiasm characterized the Jerusalem visited by Jesus. The volume of religious talk ranged from loud to boisterous. People made faith a public spectacle. Had radio and television existed at the time, Jerusalem stations would have carried non–stop religious programming. No doubt, media critics would have raved about "The Old Time Religion Hour" as it rapidly ascended in the Nielsen ratings. In truth, however, religion—especially gospel–oriented religion—fared poorly in Jerusalem.

Apparently scores of people in Jerusalem applied to religion the simplistic maxim spawned by pop psychologists—"Think enthusiastic and you will be enthusiastic." Almost anyone can do that. So, enthusiasm filled the religion of Jerusalem. And discretion suffered, if not died.

The people of Jerusalem relished a good parade—whether the throngs were going to the temple or to a cross. They got just as excited about the false trials involving Jesus as they had about the so–called "triumphal" welcome which they extended to Him when He entered the city. First they shouted, "Hosanna . . . Blessed is He who comes in the name of the Lord" (Matt. 21:9). Later, though, they screamed, "Crucify Him. . . . Crucify Him!" (Mark 15:13–14).

Looking back at Jerusalem sends a shudder down my spine. I know that situation well. So do many others. Jerusalem is familiar territory for a whole host of contemporary spiritual pilgrims. We prefer religious experiences which stir the emotions and excite the senses. In most segments of the religious community, people place a greater emphasis on feeling good than on thinking clearly and acting responsibly.

Everybody likes excitement. "It's contagious," declares an enthusiast. "Excitement makes churches grow," counsel the experts. To what end? For what purpose? Do those questions get lost completely in the mad rush to generate enthusiasm?

Other concerns also merit attention. Is our excitement the prelude to a celebration of goodness or to the crucifixion of it? Are we jubilantly singing "Hosanna" or passionately screaming "Crucify Him"? I like a good parade as much as the next person, but I must inquire about the relationship between a flourish of festivities and the status of faith and hope. What, if anything, does an explosion of enthusiasm have to do with real religion?

Most people, at their best moments, know the dangers of enthusiasm apart from an authentic commitment to Christ. Excitement without purpose tends to nurture rank selfishness. Personal satisfaction becomes preeminent over spiritual service. Both morality and faith are informed more by a person's glands than by his or her heart.

All of us know Jerusalem—much too well.

A PLACE OF DANGER

So what is the real story on Jerusalem? What is the best judgment that can be offered about this place of fickle faith, this situation of the soul?

Honestly, it is dangerous. This particular experiential spot traversed by the spirit is very, very dangerous. Warning signs and caution lights are appropriate here. Superficial religion is always more superficial than religious.

People who prefer tradition over revelation become prisoners of the past unwilling to follow God into the liberty and salvation of the present. Individuals who make the forms of faith more important than the substance of faith can spend their entire lives doing and saying all the right things while remaining empty at the core of their beings—only mimics of a faith which they really have never known.

When enthusiasm replaces Christ–centered commitment, anybody can be excited—jumping from one parade to another, boasting about an endless variety of new sensations. Sadly, though, the ceaselessly frenetic person is seldom devoted to anyone—thus, destined to spend a life time chasing after every novel religious idea which comes along while being cut off from the one and only source of authentic religious faith.

Fickle faith is more than an unfortunate development or a disappointment. It is destructive—deadly even. Seek to sense it. Look: Right outside Jerusalem—the site was much too unclean to be included in the city's holy precincts—Jesus is dying on a cross. He was put there ruthlessly by the same people who welcomed Him royally a few days earlier, when He came into town riding on a donkey. Listen: Hear the bombastic silence. Feel: Brave the chill, not of the breeze but of the deed. Think: Ponder this situation as carefully as possible—the devastation and the senseless destruction of innocence by folks claiming to be religious.

Surely someone will say, "We can't let this happen again!" And the speaker will really mean what he says. *Good*, I find myself thinking, *I refuse to be a part of such a demonic debacle disguised as religious devotion. I do not want to embrace within my soul this place called Jerusalem—a putrid spot where faith and piety cannot be distinguished from selfishness and hate.*

Movement is essential. Getting away from this place called Jerusalem in the geography of the soul is pressing. I want to live where faith is more certain as well as substantive. I desire a loyalty to Christ which lasts longer than one brief, parade–filled Sunday afternoon. If someday life can be that way in Jerusalem, great. But it is not right now.

We had best be going from Jerusalem for several reasons. Chief among them, though, is the fact that, if I have understood the story correctly, even now Jesus is coming to us.

14

BETHANY: A PLACE OF REFLECTION

> . . . Jesus came to Bethany.
> — John 12:1

BETHANY IS NOT FAR FROM Jerusalem. Geographically, it is less than two miles away. Spiritually, it seems even closer than that—a lot closer.

Jesus made Bethany His resting place during the chaotic, final week of His last Passover visit to Jerusalem. Neither rest nor reflection was possible among the throngs of pilgrims who had crowded into the holy city. Someone always had a question for Jesus. "What was that you said about Caesar?" "Are you serious about trying to destroy the temple?" "What do you believe about the Torah?" Critics and interrogators took aim on Jesus with a relentless barrage of negative comments. People would not let Jesus alone. Everybody seemed to want something from Jesus.

Even the essence of the city of Jerusalem cried out to disturb Him. The temple was rotten to the core. Priests were upset. Political passions were out of control. Rumors ran wild. Stares were harsh. The condition of the holy city disappointed Jesus—and severely saddened Him.

Jesus made no effort to avoid the turmoil of these days. He entered Jerusalem knowing full well what lay ahead of Him. Controversy was necessary. Conflict appeared inevitable. Jesus did not see Bethany as a place of escape, only as a place to pause. But He knew He needed Bethany.

Since the inception of His public ministry, Jesus regularly had claimed quiet times for recovery and reflection. Jesus recognized that He could not be significantly active if He were not consistently reflective. Long stretches of preaching, healing, teaching, and serving took their toll on Him. He required extended periods of praying. The pattern of the last week of Jesus' ministry did not differ from that of preceding days. From Jerusalem, Jesus went to Bethany—His resting, reflecting, praying place.

Everybody needs such a place. Everybody needs a Bethany.

Though Bethany was just one more site on a long list of the many spots to which Jesus had retreated for renewal, it was special. How Jesus did enjoy Bethany! He must have breathed a long sigh of relief when He had Bethany in sight.

The little village of Bethany stood in sharp contrast to the city of Jerusalem. Jesus was well liked there. Some of His best friends in all the world resided there. Jesus carried great, good memories of prior visits to the home of Mary and Martha in this village. And no one in Bethany would ever forget the explosion of joy when Jesus called Lazarus out of the tomb. Hospitality in Bethany was unlike fellowship in any other place. Jesus liked Bethany.

Is it possible that we can do without an ingredient in life which Jesus viewed as essential? Not likely. If Jesus needed Bethany, it is a good bet that everybody needs a Bethany—a place *for* the soul and/or a place *in* the soul. Every individual must have a stopping point, a site for reflection, a location for renewal. If such a place cannot be found in the world, it certainly must exist in the soul.

Why? What is so important about Bethany? What occurred there with Jesus that must find repetition elsewhere for all who long to be spiritually healthy? These are good questions, questions which have answers.

A PLACE OF CONVERSATION

Conversation took place in Bethany, for sure. Jesus enjoyed visiting with the residents of Bethany. During His stays there, He had established a pattern of open, honest dialogue with the people.

Jesus was wearied by so many words, drained physically and emotionally. Strangers had broadsided Him with a barrage of questions. They hurled each inquiry at Him like an animal trap teetering on the brink of slamming shut, needing only the slightest trigger of an unacceptable answer. Jesus had to think carefully and choose His words thoughtfully. Talk was prolific in Jerusalem. Genuine conversations, however, were absent.

Words can be so beautifully helpful or so barbarically destructive. A word can encourage or discourage, hurt or heal, enliven or kill. In Jerusalem, people talked *to* Jesus, hurling comments and questions *at* Him. In Bethany, people talked *with* Jesus.

I treasure few moments more than those spent in meaningful conversations with good friends. Such is the substance of some of the best memories of my life. Cautious comments offered with guarded emotions are unnecessary. Friends appreciate honesty. They are not put off by revelations of anxiety and fatigue or even by confessions of mistakes—large or small—and sins. Conversations among friends allow the kind of self-expression that is therapeutic—a balm for healing. I know individuals with whom I can talk for five minutes and be worn out completely. But, thank God, I know other people with whom I can talk for hours and feel refreshed.

For Jesus, Bethany was a place for conversations with friends which resulted in renewal. Reminiscing about what had been was intermingled with anticipating what would be. As Jesus and His friends recalled the pleasure of His previous visits to Bethany, they also assessed the prospects of His next day's return to Jerusalem. That kind of dialogue was essential for Jesus.

That kind of dialogue is essential for all of us.

A PLACE OF INVESTIGATION

Investigation was another important component of Jesus' visit to Bethany. Anyone familiar with the rhythm of Jesus' ministry could have predicted His trip there (or to a similar place known by some other name).

Since the earliest days of His public actions, Jesus periodically had sought out a place to pause for an examination of Himself and an evaluation of what He was doing. Many people fear such times of reflection and introspection, but not Jesus.

Immediately after His baptism, Jesus retreated to the desert for a period of intense self–examination. He also visited Caesarea–Philippi and the peak known as the Mount of Transfiguration for such a purpose. To be sure, there were other sites as well.

Within the privacy of His own soul, Jesus again explored the tension between his humanity and divinity. Perhaps He pondered and sought to answer heaven–directed questions: *Is my self–understanding correct? Are my public words and deeds consistent with the divine will? Is my pace acceptable or do I need either to slow down or to move on with more speed?* Jesus could not go for long periods of time without finding a place to deal with these kinds of questions. He would not have done so even if He could have. Jesus needed the time with God.

Sometimes, as earlier at Caesarea–Philippi—Jesus asked other people to accompany Him to a place of investigation. He never dodged honest discussion; rather, He invited it. Jesus probed His disciples with tough questions: "What are people saying about me?" "What are you hearing that I don't hear?" "How are people responding to my teachings?" Jesus wanted to know the correct answers to these inquiries. No one would be doing Him a favor by telling Jesus only what they thought He wanted to hear.

Confronting tough, discomforting questions about ourselves and our actions is very important. Most people get into serious difficulties, not because they fail to find the right answers to their questions, but because they do not raise the correct questions. In a business decision, an individual can ask, "Will this involvement be financially profitable?" when the most important issue to be resolved requires asking, "Is my participation in this venture morally responsible?" Finding an answer to the inquiry, "What do people think of what I am doing?" is not nearly so important as establishing an honest response to the question, "Am I being obedient to God's will?"

We can live without answers to all of our questions. However, to stop asking questions, to cease pushing for the realizations that come by pondering the right questions, that is to flirt with tragedy.

Lazarus would be honest with Jesus. From this long–time friend, Jesus could get much–needed information. Mary and Martha would be as quick to tell Jesus their own opinions about His work as to pass along to Him accurate reports about the thoughts of others. At Bethany, friends would level with Him compassionately and helpfully. What a priceless asset. Jesus could count on it.

A Place of Reflection

Of course, Jesus knew that in the final analysis He would have to be honest with God alone. Everybody does. Bethany was an important stopping place for Him in route to that moment. Conversation and investigation in Bethany were complemented by reflection.

Reflection also was essential for Jesus. It always had been. Retracing the footsteps of Jesus makes one aware that He did not wait until those pressure–packed hours alone in Gethsemane on the evening of the Passover to reflect and pray about His fate. Most likely, the prayers of Jesus lasted long into the night for weeks, if not months or years, prior to that last week in Jerusalem. One thing is sure. Bethany was a place of prayer.

Bethany—a place of reflection—enabled Jesus to keep His ministry in focus. Jesus had to be fully aware of the direction of His ministry, the nature of God's will, the meaning of people's reactions to Him, the maturity of His followers, and the reservoir of strength within Him. This required careful reflection gained by spending time at a Bethany place.

At Bethany Jesus' thoughts may have turned to the clash between popular Messianic expectations and resolutions shaped by the Scriptures and divine direction as perceived just after His baptism. By no means was this the first time Jesus had faced this conflict of wills, and it would not be the last time. Within a day or two, in fact, the conflict would again reach a fever pitch.

Long ago Jesus' messianic ministry was patterned after the prophet Isaiah's portrait of the suffering servant. His very affirmation of a servant ministry was at the same time a rejection of all methods of reaching people which would require Him to function as a warrior, a king, or an exhibitionist. Jesus probably reached those conclusions while in the wilderness—a lonely place.

Now though, while at Bethany, all of the previously theoretical possibilities may have returned to tempt Jesus as actual opportunities. Scores of people were ready to support His pursuit of royalty. Likewise, all the necessary ingredients were present for Him to establish Himself as a warrior without peers or as a miracle worker like no other. Did His earlier decision still stand? After all, it was made a long time ago, and things had changed dramatically since then. Amid the comforts of Bethany Jesus could see possibilities which He did not realize amid the heat of the desert.

The dilemma of Jesus required reflection by Jesus. As a result of serious reflection Jesus could come to a renewed conviction. He would continue what He started. He would do His redemptive work as a servant—even if this meant assuming the role of a suffering servant.

How important is the resolution that grows out of prayerful reflection? What if Jesus had ignored the need for reflection? What if, perhaps in a moment of weakness, He had succumbed to the push of the militarists? Might Jesus then have been killed in a meaningless skirmish with a few Roman soldiers? Reflection was essential. Thank God for Bethany.

Reflection is essential. Every person must find his way to Bethany. Few, if any, of the major issues of life are put to rest forever as a result of a one-time engagement with them—to remain single or to marry, to stay married to the same spouse or to end the relationship, to continue in one line of work or to seek another, to be involved in a local church as a leader or to retreat from organized religion altogether. Crucial decisions which affect the direction and the quality of all our days keep popping up again and again.

Authority repeatedly emerges as a major concern for most people. *Who is in charge of my life? Whom will I allow to give direction to my life? Who is creating the mold into which I am trying to fit myself?* Attention to these matters can be ignored or delayed only at a risk of great peril. Reflection is essential. Everyone needs a Bethany.

A PLACE OF CONFIRMATION

Confirmation came in Bethany—confirmation of the nature, scope, and direction of Jesus' ministry. What happened in Bethany might have sent Jesus' mind racing backwards. Perhaps He remembered His experience that distant day at the Jordan River. Immediately after His cousin baptized Him, a voice from the heavens announced divine pleasure with Him. God affirmed the being of Jesus as well as what Jesus was doing. Only recently, He had heard the voice of affirmation—the same voice heard earlier in the waters of the Jordan River—on the summit of Mount Hermon.

A woman of the streets rushed into Jesus' presence and poured perfume on Him. She used a whole flask of costly ointment on Jesus. Why?

Several of the people gathered in the room with Jesus scoffed at the behavior of this tramp: "Who does she think she is? Who does she think He is?" Jesus said nothing immediately. He knew what was going on. He was grateful for the clarity provided by this woman's action.

The woman from the streets had anointed Jesus. He had no doubt as to why. Through this one woman, perhaps a despicable prostitute scorned by the public, God was speaking. "You are on the right path. Go again to Jerusalem. This is my will." The sign was also one the people gathered in that place would surely remember later.

A PLACE OF TEMPTATION

Not everything was positive at Bethany, though, not for Jesus. It never is for anybody really. Temptation is virtually inevitable at Bethany.

Subtlety can be a serious problem in relation to temptation. Jesus knew exactly what He was up against during those forty days in the wilderness. Temptations came at Him, without disguise. He was locked into a mortal struggle with evil. But that was not the case in Bethany. Perhaps the musings in His mind during His stay in Bethany carried no suggestion of temptation. Perhaps no one would associate His thoughts— His very presence—directly with temptation. But what is not known can hurt a person—badly.

Surely Jesus measured the comfort of Bethany with the conflict in Jerusalem. If Jesus remained in Bethany, His teaching ministry could continue as in the past. The people He encountered in Bethany seemed eager to learn from Him. Besides, He was always able to relax in this place. Jesus was tired. He needed rest as well as affirmation. His death was inevitable; the actual dying could wait. Jesus could stay in Bethany, live longer, and continue His ministry.

Great temptations cloak themselves in impeccable logic. "Sound thinking" often serves as the rationale with which to justify wrongdoing. *This makes sense. Everybody will understand. Most other people have gone through the same thing.* So the reasoning goes. More often than not, wrong choices can be made to look good and sound right.

Whether or not Jesus said the words aloud, at Bethany He probably once again faced the necessity of declaring, "Get behind me, Satan!" Even the very best of places, like Bethany, can become sites of great temptations. As a matter of fact, sometimes a direct correlation exists between the level of comfort one enjoys in a place and the intensity of the temptation encountered there.

Unmistakably Bethany constitutes another stopping place in Jesus' pilgrimage which parallels a focal point in the geography of a person's soul. I know that is true for me. Though faithful discipleship often must withstand struggle and conflict, that is not the whole story. The God who calls people into engagements with difficulties also summons people to places of peace. Occasionally individuals have to make their way to spots apart, sites intended to provide distance, so as not to be drained, blinded, or mistaken in the midst of their demanding journeys.

Everybody needs conversations with loving people, honest dialogue with people who care. Investigation and reflection are crucial in the life of all people. We must not hesitate to ask ourselves crucial questions. *Am I on the right track? Am I doing God's will? How should I negotiate the troubles that dominate the path immediately ahead of me?*

Confirmation is such a great gift. But temptation is sure to come. The two phenomena often travel together. The better our experiences, the more likely temptation is to occur in the midst of them—the temptation to make a home where everything is comfortable; to cease any involvement in struggle, even the struggle required for growth; to make peace with misfortune, especially if the misfortune belongs to others; to sit back and let well enough alone. Confirmation from God provides the invaluable assurance needed to support the continuation of a responsible life.

Bethany is a good place to visit, but not to stay. People had best not pitch their spiritual tents in Bethany. It is another interim place like Egypt, a reflective spot like the desert. God does not call people to settle into perpetual retreat. Bethany should not be seen as a permanent home.

Jesus could not stay in Bethany. He had to go back to Jerusalem. And we had best be going too. God knows where literally, *God* knows where!

A world filled with hurting people cries out for help. Individuals long for redemption. Evils need to be challenged, if not eradicated. Justice requires support. Advocates beg for assistance. We had best be going.

From reflection comes a sense of reality about what is ahead. From divine confirmation comes a promise that stills threatening fears. The precedent of Jesus' pilgrimage creates within us an anticipation of encountering something surprisingly good further along the road. We must not remain in Bethany too long. Even if a cross looms large on the horizon toward which we move, confidence remains that there is more, more than we can see—a "more" which God alone can define.

Even knowing all of that, it is still tough to walk away from Bethany. It is not what we see there, but what we feel. The lay of the land does not attract us, but rather the presence of good friends and time to enjoy them.

15

THE TEMPLE: A PLACE OF REVOLUTION

And Jesus entered the temple of God . . .
— Matthew 21:12

I F JERUSALEM WAS THE HOLIEST city in the world, the temple in Jerusalem was the holiest building in the world, the holiest site in the holy city.

Only in the temple in Jerusalem could one find members of the pure priesthood appointed by God. That was the assertion of first century Jews. And, according to popular beliefs, only these temple–based priests could offer a sacrifice for all the people which would be acceptable to God, thus gaining forgiveness from God or achieving fellowship with God. Nowhere but in the temple in Jerusalem was there a site so holy that it was called "the holy of holies." This small, veil–enclosed sanctuary of mystery occupied the center of the temple. God dwelt in the temple. At least, that is what people said, and most folks considered the "holy of holies" to be the abode of God.

Architecture reflected theology in Jerusalem. The temple compound was constructed atop a mount which rose abruptly from deep valleys and towered over streets, houses, and businesses. It dominated the city—physically and spiritually. Impressive, intimidating walls surrounded this symmetrically proportioned one-thousand-square-foot structure. Terrace upon terrace thrust the temple skyward. Snowy marble and glittering gold capped the building as a crown. On a clear day, the rays of the sun reflected off the pinnacle of this structure. The very appearance of the temple communicated the presence of the omnipotent, majestic God.

For Jewish people, the temple was the nexus of their history, religion, nationalism, and hope. If the temple was somehow removed from their lives, life itself would begin to come apart.

Several years ago, the Archbishop of Canterbury asserted that the world can be saved from chaos and collapse only by the worship of God. Jewish people in the time of Jesus understood such a conviction. For them, the worship of God stood at the center of life. That is why the place of worship, the temple, was so important.

In the minds of many people today, both the Archbishop's assertion and the early Jewish conviction might qualify as gross overstatements—if not outright misstatements—of truth. In many segments of contemporary society, neither the word "worship" nor the concept of worship gives rise to any sense of grand significance.

Worship. Hearing the word prompts me to recall images from innumerable Sunday morning experiences. The music selections have received mixed reviews. Some songs made people feel comfortable or gave them a thrill; almost everybody liked those selections. However, other pieces of music seemed too slow, too "high brow," or too long; people complained about those works. No one sermon stands out, though one or two good pulpit stories can be recovered. Mostly, though, the entire Sunday morning "worship hour" seems to run together––the prayers, the hymns, the sermons.

To be perfectly honest, what people tend to remember most about worship services matters least—a man who is notoriously late to every service, a lady who wears outlandish hats, the babies who always cry about something, the children who rush out of the sanctuary to go to the bathroom, and a likable fellow who always prays exactly the same prayer every time. Sad to say, countless people have departed from innumerable Sunday services without an awareness of being any better off than when they arrived.

The reality of this situation causes us to question the remark of the Archbishop and the conviction of the Jews regarding the centrality of worship in life. Worship cannot even keep some people awake, much less affect a redemptive change in the world.

Wait, though. We may be working with the wrong images. Perceptions of worship and what the Bible depicts (and Jesus commends) as worship may be as far apart spiritually as the northernmost point and the southernmost point of Palestine are physically—further probably.

A PLACE OF WORSHIP

The essential nature of worship comes clearly into focus as you retrace the footsteps of Jesus, especially as He made His way into the temple immediately before His final Passover observance. To rethink the experience of Jesus in the temple may help us understand the significance of a worship center in our souls.

As Jesus approached the temple, He saw the lofty walls surrounding the outer court. Making His way into the place of worship by way of one of the eight gigantic gates cut into the fortress–like walls, Jesus probably noticed the costly gifts from foreign potentates which adorned the porches of the temple. Just beyond the large double colonnades which surrounded these porches stood the Court of the Gentiles.

Jewish people considered the Court of Gentiles a profane place. Here they marketed birds and animals to be used in temple sacrifices, erected sales booths for temple–related articles, and exchanged money across large tables. Many foreign Jews milled around in this area, waiting to enter the inner courts of the temple. Arguments raged. Loud bargaining echoed against the stones. Sheep, oxen, pigeons, and other potential sacrifices did what cramped or caged birds and animals do. The entire area reeked with the feel, sights, scents, and sounds of a huge bazaar.

Oh, religious words were heard there. However, the sounds of religion do not guarantee the presence of religion. Competing salespeople hawked their various goods. They appealed to spiritual motivations, drew from a religious vocabulary, and pleaded for ritual rightness. But their goal was to make a quick denarius, not enhance anyone's worship of God.

However, the Court of Gentiles was the only place in the temple precincts where a non–Jewish person could pray and worship God. The low wall which enclosed this space stood as a line beyond which no Gentile or unclean person dared to go. Signs warned Gentiles that they could lose their lives by going beyond that point.

In this outer court of the temple, manipulation was more in evidence than inspiration. Profit–taking was more apparent than covenant–making. In fact, a Gentile, or any person for that matter, would really have to work hard to find a way to pray here in this house of prayer.

What Jesus expected when He walked into the Court of the Gentiles, we can only assume. What He actually saw, though, is a matter of record. Between the press of the people crowded into this area, Jesus could see the benches provided for those wanting to talk together or to pray. No one was using them, though. Who could pray with the babble all around? Jesus saw salespeople where worshipers should have stood. Instead of calm and people lost in wonder, love, and praise—in the worship of God—He heard a noisy roar from the frenzy of buying and selling.

What a sad picture. What a disturbing situation. And it can happen to any place of worship—the temple in Jerusalem or a crowded, noisy spot in our souls—meant to focus on the worship of God.

Suddenly Jesus flew into a rage, rebuking the counterfeit friends of faith and overturning their sales booths and displays. Tables fell. Bird feathers filled the air as frightened pigeons flew out of broken cages. Escaping animals threatened to trample anyone in their way. The crowd reacted with shouts of rage. No doubt, too, people looked at Jesus in disbelief. Who would dare cause such chaos anywhere, especially in the temple?

But what happens at the worship place in our souls? What happened when Jesus entered the temple at Passover time in Jerusalem? Look carefully. Jesus' behavior in the temple communicated the importance of the worship of Almighty God. Jesus demonstrated the truth that God will not tolerate anything which detracts from the importance of worship, erodes the value of worship, compromises the practice of worship, or infringes on the work of worship. We had best not put up with it either.

Of course, the temple in Jerusalem had no monopoly on a sickness made to look like righteousness, profiteering disguised as service, piety as a shield for self-interest. What fills our places of worship? The ones down the street from where we live? The ones in our hearts?

At stake in the worship of God is far more than a recital of our contributions to a local religious radio station, our support for a corporation determined to employ only Christians, our conformity to sacred traditions, or our display of an impressive spiritual demeanor. The most important criteria for evaluating a place of worship has little to do with singing a new hymn or patting your feet to an old familiar gospel song, with the eloquence of the person in the pulpit, with the comfort of the chairs, or with the temperature of the room. In the worship of God, all that matters is how a person relates to God.

By way of His uncharacteristically volatile actions, Jesus demonstrated that causing chaos in a place of worship to bring about change is preferable to accepting a situation devoid of true worship. Regardless of tradition or popularity, routines which keep us from worshiping God meaningfully are dead wrong—and both adjectives are important: dead and wrong!

When the temple becomes a hindrance to the worship of God or threatens to become the object of worship itself, change must occur—even if the change precipitates anger and pain.

In a place of worship, talk about ministry cannot be substituted for ministry and go unquestioned. The busyness of worship and the business of worship must not supplant the substance of worship without facing a major challenge. As Jesus' example demonstrates, a place of worship must not be allowed to continue "as it has always been" *if the place no longer fulfills its God–centered purpose.*

A PLACE OF REDEMPTIVE REVOLUTIONS

The temple is a place of revolution. Either the temple is a site of the kind of worship of God which results in redemptive revolutions in people's lives, or the temple needs to be revolutionized.

A person should not always walk away from a worship center with an other–worldly gaze, whistling some cute holy tune. Look at Jacob hobbling away from Jabbok Ford after a night–long wrestling match with God. See Isaiah rocked by grief and overwhelmed by the challenge of crisis as he slips out of a smoke–filled place of worship. Study the picture of Jesus walking away from the temple in Jerusalem on that particular day.

People who can saunter into a church building, almost thoughtlessly go through the motions of regular routines, and semi–consciously mouth supposedly holy phrases had better be careful. If what takes place in our worship center is not the most important activity in our lives, we had best ready ourselves for a spiritual struggle. The temple is a place for a showdown because Jesus does not deal gently with anything or any person disruptive of the worship of God.

Where does that leave us? What does this look at the temple in Jerusalem say about our souls' choice of worship places? With God's help, we either will rid ourselves of all that stands between us and absolute devotion to God, or that which is destroying our worship will destroy us. Revolution of one kind or another is inevitable in an authentic temple.

Of course, revolutions are never cheap or easy. The emotions which Jesus stirred up in the temple in Jerusalem early that week set in motion the events of the end of that week. Reactions to the revolution which He began in the temple sent Jesus to a cross.

That is how important worship—and a place of worship was to Jesus, important enough to die for. Like it or not, we see a challenge to us: These observations about worship in His life cause us to question how important worship is to us and what the status of the temple is in our souls.

Predictable protests ensue, "We don't have to go to the temple to worship God. We can worship God anywhere." Of course, those statements are correct. However, Jesus knew that if worship had little chance of occurring in this special place—a temple constructed especially for worship—it could not be accomplished any better in the marketplace or anywhere else. No, people do not have to enter a church building to worship God. But if people do not regularly enter a worship center to worship God, they probably deceive themselves if they think they will be more faithful in worship elsewhere.

Jesus did not have to go to the temple to worship. Nevertheless, He regularly made His way to this place of worship. As a result, His entire life took on the nature of worship. That is why ultimately even a cross erected where people gambled and cursed became an altar on which Jesus expressed His greatest devotion to God.

In reality, the temple is not so much a place in the city of Jerusalem as it is a spot in our souls—a place of revolution; a place where the worship of God is basic and, thus, turmoil is inevitable. Real temples house life–changing revolutions.

Worship can feel like an earthquake—a soul quake. A whole series of aftershocks follow it, rattling and shaking the worship center. These aftershocks continually sweep through places of worship until God alone matters there and all people are given access to the worship of God.

God's will about worship will be done! Count on it. We either can cooperate with God and nurture worship centers in our lives or we can risk being driven out of those would–be worship places which we have abused and used for wrong purposes.

The message of Jesus in the temple may prompt us to offer to God a prayer that we would just as soon not pray: *God, make us uncomfortable, fill our lives with chaos, and rock us with revolutions—until we find the peace that comes in absolute devotion to God, the serenity associated with doing the will of God, and the comfort which is available only in the presence of God—the God whom we adore, love, and serve; the God whom we worship.*

No sooner do we say *Amen* to that prayer, than a bothersome rumbling begins in our souls. Jesus is at it again. The temple—including the one in our souls—will be a place of prayer.

Let us pray, really pray.

16

THE MOUNT OF OLIVES: A CRYING PLACE

. . .near the descent of the Mount of Olives . . .
He [Jesus] saw the city and wept over it.
— Luke 19:37, 41

I T HAD HAPPENED ONLY ONCE before, at least as far as any of the disciples knew. At that time Jesus stood talking with His dear friends Mary and Martha a short distance from the tomb of their recently–deceased brother, Lazarus. Whether it was a result of fatigue, compassion, the sheer weight of grief, or a combination of all that, Jesus cried. Tears streamed down His face. Jesus did not turn His head away to hide the sobs. He did not rub His face and cough. Jesus just cried.

Now Jesus was weeping again. His tears caught most of the disciples off guard.

To the disciples' way of thinking, everything was going much better than any of them had expected. None of the Twelve had anticipated the people's reaction to Jesus' arrival in Jerusalem. Even to dream of the festive parade with all of the trappings of a victory procession had been out of the question. Every one of them had probably braced for the worst.

Undoubtedly the disciples were overwhelmed by the way the crowds along the road greeted their Master and welcomed Him into the holy city. "Hosannas" rang out all around. Blessings filled the air. Their much-dreaded arrival in Jerusalem had actually seemed triumphal. Things were looking up. Everyone was having a good time.

But Jesus was crying. Why?

The cheers of the crowds were still ringing in the disciples' ears. Some of them had at long last breathed a deep sigh of relief. Maybe everything was going to be all right after all. Probably a few of the Twelve were jubilant. But Jesus was crying.

How often do emotional highs quickly plummet to emotional lows. Tears of sadness well up in eyes which moments earlier danced with gladness. Finally, on the day of a long-awaited promotion, a woman rushes home to share the good news and learns that her husband has been told he must undergo serious surgery. On the baby's first birthday, a phone call brings word of the death of a grandparent. Festivities surrounding a son's graduation from high school are cut short by an unexpected announcement of massive layoffs at the father's place of employment.

Jesus and the disciples knew the Mount of Olives well. The Mount of Olives was the name given to a two-and-one-half-mile-long ridge above the eastern side of Jerusalem. Jesus had several favorite spots along this high ground, familiar places to which He liked to withdraw and pray alone or to go and talk with the Twelve. In fact, immediately prior to this episode of weeping, Jesus had spoken with his disciples at one of these sites.

Journeys between Jerusalem and Bethany required crossing the Mount of Olives. The disciples had traversed this route with Jesus enough that they also knew it well. Terrain, colors, and vistas along the way that would capture the attention of a first-time traveler had become commonplace for the disciples.

This day was different, though. At a turn of the road along the central rise of the mountain's three highest peaks, a panoramic view of Jerusalem spread out before them. There, as Jesus scanned the city which lay just across the Kidron Valley, He cried.

Did Jesus see what He had not seen before? Or did He suddenly see clearly what previously seemed indiscernible? Whatever the reason, Jesus was weeping. And His crying place became unforgettable.

The disciples must have gazed at Jesus intently, noticeably uncomfortable with His tears. The disciples heard their Master's wistful comment about the holy city, "If you had known in this day, even you, the things which make for peace! But . . ." (Luke 19:42).

How terribly sad. In Jerusalem, a city which means "place of peace," people did not know "the things which make for peace." The inhabitants of Jerusalem refused to be gathered into the lasting security of Jesus' loving embrace. Jesus was talking about the people of Jerusalem like a distraught mother who watches her children walk straight into serious trouble and tries desperately to summon them away from danger and into the shelter of her arms. Jesus was crying.

We know. Unexpectedly, we remember a place—a dorm room, a skyline, an office, a county courthouse, a familiar neighborhood. Jesus continues to speak. Now, however, instead of Jerusalem, He seems to be speaking to Atlanta or Chicago or Omaha or Los Angeles or my home town or your home town. For Jesus continues to speak—and to cry.

This truth from the gospel really makes some people uncomfortable. "People of faith always think positively," they say. Anytime the question is asked, "How are you?" the proper cultural—not scriptural—response always is, "Great. Terrific!"

People in search of spiritual approval think they must squelch negative emotions, remain silent about terrible problems, and fight back tears under ugly conditions. Somewhere, sometime, somebody planted the poisonous seed of a horrendous idea which took root and blossomed into the lethal assumption that Christianity has no room for a crying place. It is a lie!

Jesus cried. *Jesus*—the Son of God, the Son of Man, the Savior of the world, King of kings, Lord of lords—cried. Standing nearly two hundred and fifty feet above Jerusalem, viewing the city and its inhabitants, contemplating the culmination of His mission, Jesus cried.

At that moment, Jesus could not have passed an exam or graduated from a course on the power of positive thinking. He was not "putting up a good front." For Jesus, honesty was more important. The truth came first.

Of course, much more is involved here than a specific stopping place along a tree–lined route winding down the side of Mount Olivet, a good observation point high above Jerusalem. A crying place occupies a prominent position along the expanse of the human soul. And it is not a place to be avoided. Tears are no denial of faith. Emotional hurt is not antithetical to spiritual health, not by a long shot.

A PLACE OF CONSCIENCE

To retrace the steps of Jesus along the contours of a soul requires more honesty than most people want to consider. No superficial stuff has any rightful place on this pilgrimage. Masks must be taken off and facades torn down. The journey cannot be beneficial if we cannot be truthful. Jesus' tears can help us see this truth. From Jesus we can learn that it is all right, even good, to cry.

Crying gives expression to the deepest sentiments of the heart. Weeping, like laughing, is integral to the makeup of a whole person. People who refuse to cry become less human. To fight back tears deadens life rather than enriches it.

Crying can be a matter of conscience as well as a concern of the heart. In some circumstances, not to cry seems unconscionable. When betrayal rips loving relationships asunder, tears are in order. When a senseless act of violence takes the lives of innocent people, weeping should be present. When a child is deprived of basic nutritional foods, crying seems so natural. In these kinds of situations, an absence of hurt indicates that people do not matter. And when people do not matter, God help us all!

Moved by compassion, Jesus cried over severed relationships. At times, He also cried out of conscience: He was saddened because of a creation in disarray, a city bent on immorality, and people in a hurry to get away from true joy and real love. Tears are in order when we see people who have sold out to success and sacrificed integrity for popularity—and

169

also when we see homeless people. How can any person look at prejudice and abuse and hold back cries of anger, shouts of outrage, and tears of sadness?

What kind of people can take everything and everybody in stride, never get ruffled, and never weep? God forbid! Jesus cried.

So should we. Tears well up in our eyes as we read the front page headline of a local newspaper: Five hundred people lost their jobs when a factory closed; the number of teenage suicides continues to increase; scandal ruined the reputation of a popular community leader. Weeping accompanies every step as a young woman paces back and forth in a waiting room adjacent to the critical care unit in a hospital where her best friend is dying of cancer. Dishonesty on the part of a business associate causes tears to cascade down a woman's face. Muffled sobs shake a man when he learns that members of his church voted to withdraw financial support from a mission to the street people in their community.

A PLACE OF HONESTY

Almost without exception, a person who cannot cry is a person who cannot laugh. Crying and laughing come from the same spot in a human soul. Individuals who steel themselves against weeping ultimately so deaden their lives that they lose a capacity for rejoicing. The grand hallelujahs prompted by a resurrection come to people who know the pain–inflicted tears produced by a crucifixion.

Incidentally, the same people who are most uncomfortable with thoughts of Jesus' crying also have problems with the idea of Jesus' laughing. Remember Cana? They equate holiness and blandness. They incorrectly commend mediocrity and passivity as marks of spiritual maturity.

Neither laughing nor crying is a denial of the other. Persons of faith—followers of Jesus—have the capacity for either, for both. The Gospel embraces a triumphal entry and a despicable exit, a glorious resurrection and a horrible crucifixion, uncontrollable laughter and irrepressible tears. Plotting a geography of the soul means discovering a crying place and a laughing place, a place for hurt, and a place for rejoicing. As a matter of fact, the way to one often leads straight through an experience of the other.

To be acceptable in the sight of God and welcome among the people of God, we do not have to have life all together, to always have smiles plastered on our faces, and verbalize a positive outlook. Tears are alright. Reaching out to God, it is okay not to be okay. Jesus did not come to help only people who need no help—if such a creature exists. God goes first to those with the greatest hurts every time.

In the life of Jesus and in the experience of every healthy soul, a crying place can be found. It is on the map in Palestine. It is in the soul of each individual. At the foot of the Mount of Olives, behind a desk in an office, beside an open grave in the cemetery, in the exit of a divorce court, inside a crowded detention center for illegal aliens—crying places are everywhere.

At a crying place a person can make life–changing discoveries. One is never alone there. Even while we are wiping away at our tears and trying to dry our faces, Someone meets us, greets us, and promises to stay with us. Someone knows the intensity of our hurt and the depth of our pain. That Someone also cried. That Someone is Jesus.

See you there.

17

THE UPPER ROOM: A PLACE OF DECISION

". . . a large, furnished, upper room; prepare . . . there "
And when the hour had come, He [Jesus] reclined at the table, and the apostles with Him.
— Luke 22: 12, 14

THE UPPER ROOM WAS IN Jerusalem somewhere. Actually it is just down the street from everywhere. Why bother with a second look? If you had seen one upper room, you had seen them all.

Most likely the disciples had passed the location of this guest room numerous times. No one even thought much about it, much less noticed it. What is one more guest room? Jerusalem was full of them.

Every house in the city with two rooms had an upper room. Family members sometimes prayed in these places. Infrequently a rabbi used an upper room to meet with his students. Mostly, though, a household used its upper room for storage. Given an absence of guests, worn–out sandals and dusty garments commonly filled an upper room.

One upper room looked pretty much like another. The appearance was that of a small box constructed atop the flat roof of a larger box. Outside stairs made an upper room accessible to people from the street. A typical upper room was not much more to look at inside than outside. Usually the prettiest part of the structure was a garden growing on its roof which rested on several slender pillars. But the beauty of the rooftop greenery could not be seen from the inside—or from the street below.

The room to which Jesus brought His disciples likely was furnished with a table about eighteen inches off the floor. Several mattresses or pillows were scattered on the floor around the table, providing a comfortable place for people to sit or recline. Lamps attached to the walls and hung from the ceiling provided light for the room. But decor, furniture, and outward appearances do not determine the significance of this upper room.

A similar spot can be found within a person's soul. It is an empty place which does not seem to have anything to do with religion. Certainly no one in any way would associate this open space with Jesus. It is just a room used primarily for storage. We know it well. The familiar spot is like an ordinary emotion or an open mind. We would argue that we own it. At least, we assume we are in charge of it. And, we are sure that no correlation exists between this part of our lives and anything remotely spiritual.

When Jesus sought the use of an upper room in Jerusalem, much more was involved than securing a setting for the tradition–rich ceremony of the Passover. The end was near, at least for Jesus. He needed a place to talk with His disciples about what was going to happen. Jesus wanted to participate with His friends in a very old tradition. However, Jesus also intended to use this occasion to begin something radically new.

Everybody needed to eat the Passover meal. So every effort was made to guarantee places for all pilgrims in the city to participate in this important celebration. At Passover time, Jewish residents of Jerusalem were obliged to welcome total strangers into their dwellings. Pilgrims who had journeyed to Jerusalem for this special feast filled the city. Many of these individuals had no place to stay and little, if any, food to eat. Thus, Passover visitors to Jerusalem were encouraged to ask permanent residents of the city for food and shelter during their stay. And these requests were to be granted graciously.

The upper room is a place of decision. In fact, this place does not even become important unless a decision is made to invite Jesus into it. Who would imagine that a common upper room like hundreds of others in Jerusalem would be considered a place of significance in religious history? This particular upper room has been preserved as a vital part of the biblical record only because Jesus entered that space and spent a Passover evening there.

Where is that spot in our lives? What part of my existence remains unopened to Christ even though He has viewed it as a guest room and requested entrance into it? Has Jesus sent word that He is ready for the use of a special place within the structures of our experience?

How to respond to the fundamental question of life—"Do I accept Christ or do I not?"—is not the only decision which demands a person's attention in matters of faith. The owner of the upper room in Jerusalem—possibly the mother of John

Mark—had welcomed Jesus into the household. Each of the twelve men who gathered with Jesus there had responded positively to Jesus' invitation to discipleship. Yet several other important decisions still had to be made in that upper room. And many of those same decisions still have to be made in the spaces of our hearts.

A PLACE OF SERVICE OR SUPERIORITY

Jesus entered the upper room fully aware of a disturbing tendency among His disciples. From time to time, He had overheard them debating the issue of greatness. He did not like what He heard. On one or two occasions Jesus had joined the disciples' discussions and addressed the subject straightforwardly. But He knew that a proper resolution of the matter still remained in doubt. Each one of His followers seemed dangerously pulled between superiority and service.

Jesus understood the dilemma. He had undoubtedly experienced it personally—and always chose servanthood. But that was His decision. He could not make the disciples' decision for them, any more than He will make it for us. Each has to resolve the dilemma individually.

On this particular Passover evening, the scarcity of His time made their decision about superiority and service more critical than ever. The upper room was the place for this decision to be made. Jesus knew what lay immediately ahead of Him and the disciples. Soon He would be gone. He knew that the disciples would face problems in the next few days.

Why do persons clamor so to claim a one–upmanship in relation to an individual recently deceased? I do not know, but they do. Jesus realized that after His death the disciples would begin such a discussion about their individual relationships with Him. Anyone who has spent any time at all around a funeral home can easily imagine many of the comments exchanged among the disciples: "I suppose I knew Him better than anyone else did." "Why, Jesus called me by name and spoke to me personally just last night." "I am a little reticent to point this out, but I am sure Jesus had me in mind when He talked about people being great in the kingdom." "I always thought Jesus seemed to care more for me than for some others."

If scrambles for superiority were sure to follow the crucifixion of Jesus, think what it could be like after the resurrection of Jesus. Inspired by Jesus' victory over death, his disciples would talk about Him to nonbelievers as well as to believers. Feelings of vindication would replace fears. Reticence would give way to openness in speech. Again, it is not difficult to imagine the boasts the disciples could have made: "We were with Him!" "There. See what you missed. I told you that you should have followed Him." "Jesus is going to set up His kingdom now and all of us who were loyal to Him will have a special place in it." "Who knows, Jerusalem may become the capital of the world. And I am a personal friend of the new ruler."

Jesus may have anticipated the strong possibility of difficult problems. From the beginning of their ministry together, Jesus had taught His disciples about the importance of servanthood. But He may not have been sure they had understood that priority. He had to make at least one more effort to capture their commitment. One last lesson would be offered.

In an upper room somewhere in Jerusalem, Jesus took a water basin and a towel, knelt down, and washed the disciples' feet—one by one. No one said anything, except Peter—no surprise there. All the disciples were probably uncomfortable with Jesus' behavior. However, for Jesus, the gesture was perfectly natural, an act consistent with His entire ministry.

No one could have missed the point: "My way is a way of servanthood. Following Me is not a means of gaining sovereignty of any kind. Commitment to Me requires service to everyone in need."

Since that night in an upper room in Jerusalem, the message of Jesus has never been altered or abrogated. The same truth resonates within the upper room of every person's soul.

Superiority or service? Jesus had made His decision. The upper room was the place for the disciples to make theirs. The upper room is the place for us to make our decision as well.

Judas was still in the room during Jesus' demonstration of servanthood. Already on edge emotionally, he no doubt found it disturbing to see Someone who could reach so high stooping so low. Then, Jesus washed the feet of Judas. Perhaps that was the proverbial last straw for him; he could stand no more.

All along Judas likely had thought Jesus underestimated His own strength. Now, no question about the matter remained. Jesus could be a king if He wanted to be. Why did He not use His power? Judas was ready for a battle for superiority, not ministry. He would support Jesus with His life if Jesus would only initiate the kind of struggle necessary to gain supremacy. But he was not going to spend one more minute catering to subservience. Probably with his feet still damp from the water lovingly applied to them by Jesus, Judas left the upper room in a huff. He had made his decision. Judas wanted sovereignty, not service.

A PLACE OF ACCEPTANCE OR BETRAYAL

Often making one major decision precipitates the need for another. Such was the situation in the upper room. Judas saw the next one coming. His exit was his answer to the challenge to follow. In relation to Jesus, though, each person has to decide between acceptance and betrayal. Everyone is capable of both—acceptance and betrayal. Look at Simon Peter. Jesus understood this reality. He tried hard to make His followers confront it.

A simple observation from Jesus became a sharp arrow of truth piercing the heart of each disciple. Jesus said, "One of you will betray Me." Maybe Judas had squirmed a little more than the others did when Jesus spoke. The rest of the disciples did not notice, though, because each one of them began nervously asking, "Is it I?"

It is interesting how all of them raised the same question. These men knew their potential for betrayal. When we are dead honest with ourselves, we also may not like what we see. But in that place, we cannot miss it. In the upper room we learn that every one of us is capable of betraying Jesus if all does not go well.

Acceptance or rejection? Judas had made his decision. The disciples were making theirs. We are making ours.

The sequence of events in the upper room in Jerusalem is indicative of an order of decision-making which gets repeated regularly. Making a decision about acceptance or betrayal in relation to Jesus follows a decision about superiority or service.

Jesus did not want anyone to follow Him under false pretenses. Throughout His ministry, Jesus carefully laid out the whole truth about discipleship for everybody to hear, see, and study. In a variety of different ways, Jesus said, "Before you make a decision about following Me, take a good look at what is involved. I am committed to servanthood. This is the way it will always be. The importance of service is non-negotiable in a relationship with Me. You will have to take Me as I am or not at all. Please understand that this resolve on my part will not change later, regardless of the pressure applied. Public opinion will not matter. My symbol is a towel, not a throne."

Decisions related to following Jesus come no easier in the upper rooms of our souls than they did in the souls of the disciples huddled together in an upper room in Jerusalem. Some people continue to follow Jesus looking for honor, not a job. Maybe all of us do this—or at least consider it—at one time or another. It is very tempting to view Jesus primarily as Someone who can help us rather than as someone who can strengthen us to help others.

This decision about acceptance and betrayal is an exceptionally tough one to make. Adding to its difficulty is the fact that a choice for acceptance must be made completely apart from any guarantees about ease, success, and other subsequent circumstances. If we only knew that following Jesus would raise our self-image, increase the number of our friends, enhance our business, and add to our bank accounts, we would not hesitate to make a positive decision about Him. But just to accept Jesus for who He is, that is another matter entirely. We begin to think that our spending just one night with Him in the upper room of our souls is enough for Jesus.

The writer of the Fourth Gospel noted that when Judas left the upper room "it was night" (John 13:30). That was not merely an observation about the time of day; it was a comment on the condition of Judas' soul.

A PLACE OF THE NEW OR THE OLD

By both His words and actions in the upper room, Jesus prompted the disciples to make still another decision. He set before these men an invitation which required them to choose between the new and the old. Immediately after participating with the disciples in the ancient tradition of the Passover, Jesus initiated a new tradition.

An observance of the Passover linked the disciples with all that was best in their Jewish past. The Paschal lamb had been slain. They had remembered and celebrated the Jewish people's exodus from Egypt. Hope tied to the divine promise of a Messiah had been reaffirmed. The people of Israel were comfortable with this tradition, for it provided a great sense of security and joy. No Jew would think of missing the Passover observance or breaking with this sacred tradition.

What about the disciples? Could they move beyond this popular tradition? Now Jesus placed that question squarely before them.

At the table in the upper room, Jesus offered to His followers a new loaf of bread and a new cup of wine. Oh, all of them had shared bread and wine many times before. This time was different from all the others though, radically different. Jesus indicated that an acceptance of this bread and wine would be an acknowledgment that the Messiah had come, indeed an affirmation of Jesus as the Messiah. Jesus offered the disciples food and drink for a new future, describing His provisions as a "new covenant."

In this simple room where they met to take a long and appreciative look back into the past, suddenly the disciples were called upon to peer into the future. That kind of challenge goes with the territory in the upper room. Salvation could be experienced immediately. Jesus was ready to usher these people into a future dominated by the reign of God. But were they ready? Are we?

To accept Jesus' summons to follow Him on an uncharted course would put an end to any security provided by the past.

Faithfully observing rituals intended to keep them sensitive to the presence of God in days gone by would be replaced. Now they would cooperate with God in the divine ministry of redemption in the present. Looking forward in hope would have to give way to living by love immediately as an obedient response to the divine will.

Could they do it? Can we? Would the disciples of Jesus be satisfied to cling to the comfort and security of the past? Or were they willing to acknowledge God was active in their midst and accept an invitation to join the Messiah in ministry—right then? Did the disciples prefer to live with only the traditions which they already knew? Or were they ready to obey Jesus' mandate which required fidelity to a new and different observance? Those issues demand resolution in the upper room—then and now.

Undoubtedly, there were other issues as well. No one can come close to recapturing all of the decisions which were made in that upper room in Jerusalem. We understand. The same is true today. Decisions of every size, shape, and degree of significance must constantly be made in the upper rooms of our lives.

Time was at a premium for the upper room occupants in Jerusalem. Jesus had to be going. A long, difficult night stretched out before Him. The disciples also had to be going. But their destinations were not yet clear. Whether or not they would go with Jesus or without Him for the rest of the evening still had to be decided. All that the disciples knew for sure was that, regardless of their wishes, they could not remain in the upper room.

Neither can we.

Superiority or service? Acceptance or betrayal? New or old? Following Jesus means making decisions involving options that are poles apart. That was how it was. That is how it is.

Jesus stands ready to assist us in our choice of a direction for the future. But He will not force a decision. Ultimately, each person has to resolve these basic dilemmas of life individually.

Jesus' next stop was nearby. Momentarily He would leave the upper room, walk quickly through the darkened streets of Jerusalem, descend into the Kidron Valley passing Absalom's tomb, cross a stream, and then turn to climb the side of the Mount of Olives. What was next for the disciples? What is the next stop for us?

Jesus is always moving ahead, making His way toward another place where His ministry of redemption will be demonstrated once more. What about us? Where are we going? Will we follow right behind Jesus or walk along with Him or go in another direction? We have to decide.

And we had best not wait too long. We can spend so much time milling about in that upper room—and trying to decide what to do next—that Jesus moves on without us. If that happens, we will have to run at break-neck speed to catch up with Him. For surely, surely, we do not want to miss spending every moment possible with Him, being served and serving.

18

GETHSEMANE: A PLACE OF STRUGGLE

> Then Jesus came with them [the disciples] to a
> place called Gethsemane.
> — Matthew 26:36

PEOPLE SPEAK OF ARMAGEDDON as the pinnacle of battle grounds, a war site like no other. They predict that the battle of Armageddon will be the epitome of struggle, the ultimate hostile engagement, the last word on conflict. Perhaps. But do not forget Gethsemane.

Compared to the struggle which took place in Gethsemane, the battle of Armageddon will appear more like a skirmish for clean–up forces than the critical engagement of a major war. Armageddon's outcome is assured. The crucial petitions in Jesus' model prayer—"Thy kingdom come, Thy will be done"—will be answered positively. We can count on it. God's reign is coming. Ultimately, evil will be defeated. Grace will prevail. God's will *will* be done. These are certainties.

But no certainties accompanied Jesus to Gethsemane, only a multitude of questions. Jesus was no role player in a dramatic charade moving toward a prearranged outcome. As Jesus knelt in prayer, His soul was tormented by a terrific struggle. Each of the Gospels record His experience there (Matt. 26:36-46; Mark 14:32-42; Luke 22:39-46; John 18:1-11).

Gethsemane is better known as an event than as a place. Both Matthew (26:36) and Mark (14:32) write of the site only in general terms, though each names the place—literally "olive press" or "olive vat"—by using a word that suggests the presence of olive trees. In the Fourth Gospel, John is more specific, describing Gethsemane as a garden (18:1).

Within the walls of the city of Jerusalem, no space was available for garden plots. However, affluent residents of Jerusalem maintained gardens on the nearby slope of the Mount of Olives. On the evening prior to His death, Jesus most likely retreated to one of these gardens in order to pray.

Gethsemane was not far from the upper room or from any other location in Jerusalem. Naturally, a place of struggle is always nearby. Jesus had only to exit Jerusalem through a city gate on its eastern boundary, cross the Kidron Valley, and then climb a short distance to a secluded spot hidden among the proliferation of trees on the Mount of Olives.

A vicious battle occurred at this place called Gethsemane. To be sure, this war within the will could have happened anywhere. Actually, it happens everywhere. Struggles of the soul are not limited to specific spots on a map.

With emotionally–volatile events swirling around Him, Jesus had to find peace. Unlike battles foretold in ancient apocalyptic literature—bloody skirmishes in which the forces

of good and evil are clearly identifiable and victory is synonymous either with the reign of God or the dominance of the
demonic—the struggle within Jesus was complex and ambigu-
ous. Not all of His choices involved clear–cut options between
right and wrong. Jesus was perhaps caught in a dilemma pitting
what was acceptable against what was good, what was better
against what was best.

A PLACE OF STRUGGLE

We know Jesus struggled as He prayed; the Gospels tell us
that. We can only imagine the diverse thoughts which might
have warred against each other within the will of Jesus during
the midnight hours which he spent in Gethsemane. Of course
our imaginings inevitably fall far short of what actually occurred there: *I am confident that Judas has gone for My captors.
If I stay here and submit to their arrest, I probably will be dead in
a matter of hours. I don't want that. Maybe I should not admit
that, though I must be honest. I want to do My Father's will. But
if I can be obedient to God without drinking the cup of death, that
is what I prefer. So much has to be considered and so much is
unknown. If I could be sure My disciples are ready to carry out the
divine mission, that would make My decision easier. But I have
real questions about them. Already one has turned on Me. Peter is
as strong as any of them, yet I am sure that before tomorrow's dawn
he is going to deny that he has ever known Me. What I see around
Me doesn't help. At this very moment, with My life hanging in the
balance, the ones to whom I have turned for support are asleep.
What will happen if I am taken from them? Who will move ahead
with all that has been started? I need time, more time. Not even
My closest associates have understood the nature of love and the*

centrality of grace. They are still thinking I will set up a new civil government here in Jerusalem. Yes, I need time.

Jesus knew Gethsemane well. He knew that the road to Jericho was easily and quickly accessible from the place where He knelt to pray. He had friends in Jericho. Also close by was the route He frequently had traveled to Bethany. Probably His best friends in the world were there. Perhaps the geographical location of Gethsemane was itself a form of temptation for Jesus. We do not know.

Perhaps He thought: *Maybe it will be best for Me to prevent a showdown right now. I'm sure it is not too late to avoid it. I need more time for teaching, preaching, and talking so people will better understand the message which God entrusted to Me. Living now to die later may be far better than submitting to death immediately and bringing everything to a halt. It will not be that difficult to just slip down the backside of the garden and return to those hospitable people in Galilee. Even if the soldiers get here before I can get away, Peter has his sword strapped to his side and the other disciples would likely welcome a fight. Who knows but that Judas might join us if he thought at long last some Roman heads were going to roll. But the matter surely can be resolved without violence. These people probably would be so glad to have Me out of town that they will do no more than rejoice if I announce that I am leaving. There is so much more good I can do.*

Does such reasoning have a ring of familiarity about it? For me, it does, whether or not Jesus had those thoughts. Many of life's greatest struggles do not involve sharply distinguished options between right and wrong but rather alternatives that have strong arguments for and against them. At a Gethsemane place, people's words differ from time to time, but the basic struggle remains the same.

Is this the moment to take my stand in this company? Should I refuse to budge another inch in holding to my convictions and risk reprimands or maybe even dismissal? I believe I need to speak. But if I stay quiet now, I can continue to do a lot of good things. Everybody will understand my not risking my livelihood to be faithful to a principle. Some think that for me even to consider speaking up is outright foolish. Though the matter seems to be a critical test of my faith right now, I am sure that with the passing of time I will see it differently.

We have all been there. Each of us has thought the same things at one time: *Oh, I am well aware of what the Bible says about forgiveness. However, I must be realistic. If I actually forgive that person and seek to establish a good relationship with him, some people are going to misunderstand. I can hear it now: A few folks will accuse Me of being "soft on sin." Grace is hardly ever understood or appreciated except by those who receive it. Why is my forgiveness such a big deal anyway? He will not be affected much one way or another by whatever I do or don't do. I am the one who stands to lose something or get hurt. Maybe it is best for me to stay away from him and not say anything. If a situation ever arises where something has to be said, I will test the opinions of others and agree with the prevalent comments. Then, if I feel the need to, maybe someday I can correct it all and make it up to him in some way.*

We know Gethsemane. The fiercest fights that rage within our souls may not be those between right and wrong but those between holding convictions and knowing the right time to express them. The worst battles raging in our souls may pit righteousness against expediency and courage against popularity. Reasons always exist—good-sounding, logical reasons— not to do the highest good: "A better moment will come." "Conditions are not right at the moment." "The issue is too confused." "The result is too controversial." "I would love to act courageously, but I must think of my job and my family." "I have to be practical as well as responsible." How we do know Gethsemane!

A PLACE OF CONFLICT

The most fundamental conflict in Gethsemane is between wills—between God's will and my will or your will. Jesus left no doubt about His will. He was as honest as usual. Jesus did not want to die. As much as He wanted to be God's agent for redemption, Jesus desired an obedience to God apart from suffering love and without His own innocent death.

Reflective judgments about other people are precarious, if not outright dangerous. A spirituality two thousand years removed from the situation in that distant Gethsemane can deceive us. After reading the passion narratives in the Gospels, someone usually thinks, *I could have done it. I can do it. If I knew the world could be saved by my death, I would submit to it in a heartbeat.* Really?

Jesus prayed to God, "Not what I will, but what Thou wilt" (Mark 14:36). The words probably did not form in His throat effortlessly or roll off His lips easily. In his account of Gethsemane, Luke says that Jesus sweat drops of blood as He spoke these words (22:44). What incredible intensity. Agreeing to obey the bidding of His heavenly Father took every ounce of energy Jesus could muster. And it had best be that way for everybody. If submission to the divine will is easy, the person involved had better look again, this time more carefully.

Anyone eager to say to God, "Not my will but as Thou wilt," should realize that the issue today may not be climbing on a cross. "Thy will be done" can mean going to an estranged neighbor and starting a conversation, seeking to kill a personal prejudice that dominates relations with people who are different, assuming a controversial posture in protest to an immoral national policy, or serving as an agent of reconciliation among rival political factions with the community. God's will can lead a person to work on a bad marriage rather than giving up on it or to reach out to a rebellious child rather than turning away in anger. Walking out to Golgotha may seem preferable to walking into the office and speaking up for what is right or seeking to live as an advocate for grace among scores of people who are more comfortable with judgment. Some things seem worse than death.

It is like sweating blood to struggle with the teachings of the Sermon on the Mount where one lives. We sometimes like to think that we could be faithful to the divine will far more easily on a mission field miles removed from our home or even in another city. *These people know me,* we think. *If I say "Your will be done" to God, who knows what that might involve? And if some bizarre deed or a form of vulnerable behavior is required, what will the home folks say about me? How will they react? I've got to keep in mind that I must go on living here.*

An individual could surmise that the crucial struggle of Gethsemane is always one of cosmic proportions. It is always a faraway place and a distant experience. No, that is not the case at all. Gethsemane is always near—just outside the gate or across a valley or down the street or up a small incline. And the struggle is always personal—very, very personal. Nobody can avoid it. Everyone has to deal with Gethsemane. Its existence is apparent in even the slightest glance at a geography of the soul. A place of struggle is a fundamental focal point for a person of faith.

The Greek writer Nikos Kazantzakis tells of a young truth seeker who traveled to a monastic community off the coast of Greece. He wanted to visit with the monks there and seek to discover their way to God. One day the young man talked with an old hermit who had lived alone for forty years. The conversation went something like this:

"Tell me, father," the seeker said, "do you struggle with the devil?"

"Oh no, my son," the elderly man responded, "my flesh is too old for that. I struggle now with God."

The young man was astonished. "With God, father? Do you hope to win?"

The wise monk replied, "Oh no, my son. I hope to lose."

Neither the cross nor the resurrection can be understood apart from what happened at Gethsemane—not in the life of Jesus and not in our lives.

Blessed are those who struggle with God and lose. Wise is the person whose constant prayer is a confession of submission, "Not my will, O God, but Your will be done."

That is what happens at Gethsemane.

19

GOLGOTHA:
A PLACE OF DEATH

> They took Jesus . . . and He went out, bearing His own
> cross, to the place called the Place of a Skull, which is called
> in Hebrew, Golgotha.
> — John 19:17

DARK, WIND-SWEPT CLOUDS rumbled across a deep gray sky. Rain fell incessantly, sometimes in sprinkles and sometimes in torrents. A chill pervaded the air. My wife and I had been told that local villagers would not give us directions to our desired destination. However, a man from Munich agreed to accompany us.

When we arrived at Dachau, our souls shivered from a cold that could not be shut out by our heavy coats. In this former prison camp, countless Jews suffered and died. As we walked through the gates of Dachau, a preoccupation with death overwhelmed me.

My feelings fluctuated wildly. I wanted to see the yards, furnaces, bunkers, and dormitories in this place of horrible atrocities. But I also wanted to run, to turn my head, to get away. I did not want to confront the fact that such an inhumane place had ever existed or to admit that inexplicable evil was a matter of reality. I wanted to forget it all. Thoughts of the senseless deaths that occurred at this site gripped my mind like the drops of water I could see clinging to the tightly–strung barbed wire around me.

The sensations I experienced at Dachau are appropriate to a visit to Golgotha, the place where Jesus was crucified, the spot where He died.

A PLACE OF A CROSS

Golgotha—a weird, rocky, skull–like plateau—was located just outside the wall of Jerusalem. A holy city could not have an execution site within its precincts. That would spoil the purity of the place. Ironic reasoning! The killing of Jesus could be plotted within the holy city, even within the sacred sections of the temple. Unjust trials for Jesus did not seem to be an abomination for anyone within Jerusalem. But the dying had to be set apart. A crucifixion could not be allowed within the city. So Jesus was placed on a cross sunk deep into a mound of earth outside Jerusalem. And all the holy people in the city went outside the city to witness the sadistic spectacle of Jesus' murder. A sizable depression immediately underneath the plateau may have given onlookers an impression that the jaws of the skull were open. Jesus died at Golgotha.

Many times it is that way. Death seems so unspiritual. Maybe that is because death is often irrational. Almost always it brutally assaults people's emotions. Everyone knows death is coming, but no one wants to think about it. Most people, even those who can cope with the deaths of others, refuse to contemplate their own deaths or the deaths of their family members. Numerous Christians refuse to reflect at any length on the death of Jesus. Usually, Golgotha is just beyond the gates.

Individuals who really like being in Jerusalem on Palm Sunday do not care much for visiting Golgotha on Good Friday. All decorations are down. Candles are no longer burning. Laughter has been silenced, as have hosannas and hallelujahs. A procession of mourners has replaced the parade of merrymakers. No longer important are the exclamations of praise. What counts now are the convictions about Jesus lodged within each person's soul.

Jesus died on a cross devoid of gold or silver plating. No beautiful lilies adorned the shaft of that cruel instrument of death. Decorations for the cross are post–Easter contributions to the art of that ignoble event. Our desire to make the cross more palatable is completely understandable—but Golgotha was not a pretty place. It never is.

Golgotha was a place of death. The end. No one who watched Jesus die entertained a thought of resurrection. Easter was not even a word in their vocabularies, much less an event embraced by their hopes. Golgotha was a place of death.

Theologians assert that a cross existed in the heart of God long before a cross was erected at this place called Golgotha. True. What I find most disturbing about that observation is its relation to a realization that accompanies it. We are created in the image of God. Think about it. A cross is in the heart of

God, and we are created in the image of God. So what is in our hearts? Anxiously scanning the terrain of my soul, I squint to see if there is anything that looks like a cross within me.

What causes crosses? What is at stake at Golgotha? Careful thought must precede a response to these inquiries. The issue is not what causes death. Everyone knows that. Diseases, accidents, a loss of will, and advanced age are causes of death. But what causes crosses?

Conflict causes crosses, but not just any conflict. Crosses are formed when the horizontal and vertical dimensions of life get at odds with each other. When the ways of God intersect the ways of humankind, a cross takes shape. And every time that happens, God suffers. Actually we do too, though our suffering may not be as immediate or apparent.

When the sinfulness of people runs headlong into the goodness of God, a cross occurs. Golgotha. When the unfaithfulness of people intersects the faithfulness of God, a cross is formed. Golgotha. When people bent on doing evil meet God who is intent on doing good, a cross is constructed. Golgotha. When people pursuing their own wills bump into God seeking obedience to the divine will, a cross is raised. Golgotha.

What happened outside the wall of Jerusalem can happen anywhere. Indeed, it does happen—everywhere. A cross protrudes from the geography of every soul as well as stands against the horizon of the ancient holy city. No one knew that truth better than the apostle Paul who confessed, "I have been crucified with Christ" (Gal 2:20) and "I die every day" (1 Cor. 15:31). Paul hosted a Golgotha in his soul whether or not he ever visited the killing place just outside the wall of Jerusalem.

A PLACE OF REDEMPTION

Most elements of death are understandable; for example, loneliness. Each person must experience death individually. No one can die for someone else and assure the other person of never having to die, never having to hurt. Everybody knows the hurt associated with death. Any severing of meaningful relationships is painful. When the disruption is permanent, grief is inevitable.

The death of Jesus was different, although I do not understand all about it. Jesus' death was redemptive, and I cannot explain that. How was the death of Jesus redemptive? Maybe it was because of the innocence of the One crucified. Perhaps the reason has something to do with the fact that by all rights we should have been there instead of Jesus. Maybe the explanation is that God willed this death. I do not know; I cannot explain it. But that does not alter the fact: Jesus' death was redemptive.

Interpreting what happened at Golgotha as redemptive is not an afterthought, intended to place the despicable event in the best possible light. Rather, evidence of redemption was immediate. When Jesus died, creation was shaken to its core. A pagan soldier suddenly blurted out a confession of faith, "Truly this man was the Son of God" (Mark 15:39).

Neither was the idea of Christ's death as redemptive a passing thought. The Gospels are full of it. Throughout history people have professed this truth, and some have even accepted death for themselves rather than deny it. Like many of my contemporaries, I know this reality experientially. By the death of Jesus, I am provided unique access into the presence of God. Golgotha is in truth a place of redemption.

This book is about stopping places in the life of Jesus which parallel spots within a human soul. At first reading, we might conclude that a treatment of Golgotha should have been omitted from this volume. We could argue convincingly that Jesus' death at Golgotha is without any counterpart in the geography of the soul. Avoid a hasty conclusion, though.

A Golgotha, a place for a cross, exists in every life. Golgotha is the place where an individual takes a crucial personal stand. The cross beams of the experience are shaped by the clashes between good and evil, right and wrong, righteousness and sinfulness that occur in everyone. Conflicts between an individual's will and God's will are the stuff that make up Golgotha. It is a place of death. At Golgotha people either take their stand with God and die, or they walk away unable ever to take a stand again. Breathing continues, but the possibility of experiencing a meaningful life is left behind, at the spot where the cross stood.

Watching the Passion Play in Oberammergau, Germany, I learned something about the end of Jesus' passion that I had previously missed. A huge crowd of people milled around the platform where officials stood with Jesus. The authorities extended an option to the throng—free Jesus or free Barabbas. Immediately shouts and cheers lifted the name of Barabbas. "Barabbas! Free Barabbas." But not all were of one voice. This is what I had missed.

Amid boisterous cries calling for the release of Barabbas, I heard the faint, almost drowned-out, sound of a few people saying, "Jesus! Release Jesus." Then I saw them, stage right. There were not many. These few people were almost swallowed up by the rest of the crowd. But they were there!

A small number of people had gathered to support Jesus and to shout their pleas for His release. Every time the throng screamed, "Barabbas," this little group shouted, "Jesus." Though at a glance, everybody in the scene seemed to want Jesus crucified, a few did not. And they said so with all of the courage and might they could muster. Strangely, never before had I thought that any supporters of Jesus had shown up in that hostile crowd.

Of course, this small band of people did not get what they wanted. They lost their vote by an overwhelming margin. Actually, they well may have known that would be the case when they showed up. But they did show up. They were present with Jesus and for Jesus until the end. They did not renounce their support for Christ just because the odds were against them. These people were creating and bearing crosses of their own. Golgotha was no unfamiliar spot for them.

The dramatists of Oberammergau helped me immensely. But their portrayal of the passion also caused me trouble. I have not been able to get that scene out of my mind. I keep asking myself, "Where would I have been? What would I have been doing? Would I have showed up? If so, what would I have been saying? Would I have screamed my support for Jesus, whispered it, or merely kept it in my thoughts?"

Golgotha is a place of disturbing, unnerving, disorienting death. But the death is redeeming! I know the difficulty of placing those two words together—*redeeming* and *death*. Yet that is the nature of Golgotha when Jesus is there.

I do not like to go to Golgotha. The thought of what happened there is bad enough; I have no desire to recall the sight. Though following in the footsteps of Jesus has great attraction to me, I must admit that this is one place on that journey that has absolutely no appeal at all. Who relishes the thought of dying for one's convictions? Who wants to be crucified between good and evil?

Still, Golgotha is a place within my soul. I am trying to learn to be grateful for that fact. Crucifixion is essential for salvation. Crucifixion is a non–negotiable if there is ever to be a resurrection. Of course, neither of those truths makes dealing with Golgotha any easier. But both make the promise of the experience better. Golgotha is a place of hope as well as death.

At a place called Golgotha, Jesus of Nazareth was crucified. While on the cross, He died.

PART IV

A Place of Resurrection and Hope

20

GALILEE:
A MEETING PLACE

He (Jesus) has risen . . .tell His disciples and Peter
He is going before you to Galilee; there you will see Him.
— Mark 16:6–7

TRAGEDY CASTS A LONG, DARK shadow across
life. Maybe the sun rose in a cloudless sky on the
Sunday morning after Jesus' crucifixion on the previous Friday, but it really did not matter. Darkness shrouded
the souls of all who had devoted their lives to Jesus. The shadow
of the cross snuffed out any light within its reach.

The unnecessary death of an innocent young person is
tragedy of the highest order. The senseless murder of a close
friend is almost more than an individual can take. But how
difficult must it have been when the young person was Jesus—

when the close friend was affirmed as God's Son, accepted as the long–awaited Messiah, and followed as Lord!

As the initial shock of Jesus' death wore off, spiritual numbness in the lives of Jesus' followers probably gave way to emotional panic. Only throbbing pangs of grief interrupted the reign of fear among them—a fear both reasonable and irrational.

Horrors from the Friday afternoon crucifixion continued to haunt Mary Magdalene and Mary the mother of James even as they made their way to the garden tomb where the body of Jesus had been laid. Questions probably tore into their consciences—one in particular: *How could such a despicably evil deed be done in a world created by a good God?* The only conclusion would rip the fabric of their security: *Life is totally unpredictable!*

The two women named Mary could not forget the death of Jesus or dismiss the questions which that death raised regarding their own lives. They had to be thinking: *What will we do without Jesus? How can we ever get back to normal lives? Nothing will ever be the same again.*

Amid the pervasive uncertainty unsettling the lives of these two women, one resolution did not waver, however. Perhaps neither Mary knew what she would do even during the rest of the day, much less in the future, but both were certain of what had to be done in the moments which followed dawn on the Sunday morning after Jesus died. They must anoint the body of Jesus.

Traveling to the tomb intended to house Jesus' body was difficult. These women did not like being around death. Nobody does. Yet they longed to do one last thing for Jesus. They intended to anoint His body with oils as a final act of compassionate devotion. As the women neared the tomb, they may very well have wanted to run in the opposite direction. However, they forced their steps to take them to the burial site of Jesus.

When they entered the tomb in which the body of Jesus had been placed, however, they were astonished. The body was not there. Instead, a messenger from God sat where the body should have been lying. As the women stared in disbelief at the emptiness of the tomb, the angel spoke to them. They received instructions which Jesus Himself had requested them to take to His disciples—"He is going to Galilee . . . there you will see Him."

Suddenly what they saw and heard sank in. *He is going to Galilee. Jesus is going to Galilee!* The two women started running; no doubt their thoughts were moving even faster than their feet. Their anxiety had quickly given way to excitement. Enthusiasm had replaced fear. Despair had been eliminated by joy.

When the disciples heard the women's story, their emotions must have been confused as well. The men wanted to believe in the resurrection—desperately wanted to believe it—but they knew about the crucifixion. They knew that Jesus had died.

Interestingly, only two of the eleven disciples actually went to the tomb themselves to check out the women's report, to be certain that the body of Jesus was not there. But all probably got ready to leave town. They knew not a minute could be wasted. They dared risk no hesitation, not even a brief delay, before heading out toward Galilee—a three-day journey from Jerusalem—and their meeting with Jesus.

What a joyful trip. We can imagine the laughter and shouts of glee as the disciples walked and at times almost ran toward Galilee. Their thoughts must have been full of their excitement: *He is alive! Jesus has been raised from the dead. We are going to see Him. Just think, we will be together again. Jesus is going to meet us in Galilee!*

What was so important about Galilee? Why did Matthew and Mark stress Jesus' statement about Galilee, place such a major emphasis on Galilee as a meeting place for the resurrected Jesus and His astonished disciples? What was the significance of Jesus designating Galilee as the place where He would get together with His companions again?

Galilee, literally the "circle," was the most populous district in the northern part of Palestine and perhaps the most beautiful as well. Moisture from the Lebanon mountains enriched the greenery of the rolling hills and lush valleys which surrounded several inviting lakes in the region. Fruits and vegetables were plentiful.

Estimates are that as many as three million people resided in the more than two hundred towns and villages which comprised Galilee. The citizenry of the district was racially diverse, due to intermarriage.

Commerce thrived in Galilee. All kinds of trade took place there. The greatest roads of the East wound their way through this district. One old saying asserted that Galilee was on the way to everywhere.

Generally, people who felt that Jerusalem was urbane and stifling viewed Galilee as inviting and invigorating. The very nature of the land seemed to inspire freshness and freedom among its inhabitants. Most Galileans were warm and impulsive people, excitable and often passionate to a fault. They were open to new ideas and willing to entertain new thoughts.

The residents of Galilee were notorious for their laxity in supporting the temple; however, they possessed a piety which made them receptive to the ministry of Jesus. Little wonder that He spent more time in Galilee than anywhere else.

Early in this century, biblical scholars discovered that in the Gospel of Mark the term "Galilee" functions as much more than a geographical designation. Not only a title for one region of Palestine, the term "Galilee" here describes a special time and a special place in the ministry of Jesus.

Reflect on the many significant experiences in the ministry of Jesus which took place in Galilee. Jesus preached powerfully there. He called His disciples in Galilee. Multitudes of people were helped by Jesus in this region. Galileans followed Jesus with an acceptance and enthusiasm unmatched elsewhere. Controversy was at a minimum in Galilee. Hope was vibrant there.

In the minds of many of Jesus' followers, Galilee had come to represent Jesus' place. Additionally, Galilee was a term which stood for familiar territory, ordinary days, common pursuits. When the messenger from God said that Jesus was going to Galilee, the disciples understood that Jesus would meet them where they knew Him best and needed Him most. The messenger was addressing us with the same truth as well.

Jesus was no longer confined to a tomb in a garden somewhere around Jerusalem. Jesus was not even restricted to the holy city. He was risen—risen from death. Jesus was alive and free to move anywhere, everywhere, as He willed. The disciples could meet Him in Galilee. The word from God's messenger meant that everything was all right.

"So what?" one of us may ask. "I don't live in Galilee. The reference has no meaning for me." Such an attitude highlights the crucial point of the narrative which is not to be missed. Galilee is everywhere. Jesus might just as well have left word for the disciples to meet Him in New Orleans, Moscow,

Teheran, or Cape Cod. He is alive and doing again what He had done before. Jesus Christ is still at the task of offering good news, calling disciples, extending grace, promising rest, and instilling hope.

A PLACE OF INVITATION

We know Galilee. It is a place of invitation—a place to which we are drawn by an invitation to meet the risen Christ.

One of the writer John Masefield's fictional characters explained the resurrection truth in terms of Jesus being "let loose" in the world. The description is by no means fiction. The risen Christ is free to be everywhere. People can meet Christ anywhere. To ponder the invitation to travel to Galilee is to realize that the essence of the Christian pilgrimage is not to be found in heated contentions about an empty tomb but in excited reunions with the risen Lord.

The messenger in the tomb of Jesus was speaking to all people, not to two women alone. The words are for everybody: "He is going to Galilee." No pressing spiritual need exists to organize a pilgrimage, catch a plane or a ship, and journey to Jerusalem. Jesus is not in any one place more than in another, not even in one considered a "holy" place. Jesus joins us where we live, while we perform daily tasks. We do not have to travel to where He was. Jesus comes to where we are.

In Galilee we know that Jesus is alive, not dead. We do not have to worry about a proper resting place for His bones. We need not build a shrine to designate the spot where He can be met. Jesus is alive. He wants no shrine. He refuses to be confined. Jesus wants to abide in people's lives.

We do not have to wait for a special season any more than for a special place to meet Jesus. The resurrection set Jesus loose in the world making all days sacred and all lands holy. "He is going before you to Galilee" (Mark 16:7), the messenger from God said. Jesus will meet us where we are anytime and every time we need Him.

One Holy Week in a German concentration camp, Heinrich Gruber etched into the gravel on the ground: "Vivit—He lives!" Later Martin Niemoeller found the words. His spirit soared. Barbed wire could keep prisoners in this hellish place, but it could not keep Christ out. Gruber and Niemoeller were being held captive in Galilee! Galilee is a place where Christ arrives to create freedom and hope amid bondage and despair.

Elie Wiesel reported a sickening event from that same horrendous period of time. In another concentration camp, officials hanged a young Jewish boy to make a point about the evil of stealing a crust of bread. When a man who was plummeted into despair by this repulsive spectacle cynically asked, "Where is God now?"— the response came, "He is hanging upon that gallows." Galilee. It is a place where Christ meets people to stand with them—or sit or hang with them—suffer with them and even die with them.

On a lonely island somewhere in the South Pacific, a missionary was forced to dig a grave for his wife. His pain was relentless and intense. Later, looking back on that day, the man explained that he never could have made it had it not been for his sense of Jesus' presence. Galilee. It is a place where Christ shows up to strengthen mourners beside the graves of loved ones, patients in surgery suites and mental health wards, and individuals in other situations involving loss.

"He is going to Galilee." The words are for us. Jesus promises to join us in Galilee where we work, play, and relate as a family. The risen Christ points us to a meeting place— whether in a line seeking unemployment compensation or in a board room making multi–million dollar decisions, on the athletic field or in a court of law. We claim the promise of the meeting place when we reach out to Christ amid difficulties in an office or as we pray in a traffic jam on the expressway.

A PLACE OF COMMISSION

We know Galilee. It is a place to which we are drawn by an invitation to meet the risen Christ. And it is a place at which we receive a commission from the risen Christ. Galilee is a place of commission.

As soon as the disciples of Jesus received word about meeting Him in Galilee, they understood the meaning of the message. *He wants us in Galilee—no more hiding out in the holy city, no more silence. Christ is risen. We must be going—to Galilee.*

Not infrequently the word Galilee had been associated with Christ's mission to the world. That association must have also been in the disciples' thoughts. *Jesus wants us to get busy doing what He taught us to do. He is alive. We are to be active as evangelists, as teachers, as prophets, and as ministers. He is going to Galilee. There we must serve in His name.*

Amazing turnarounds take place in Galilee. In the hours after the crucifixion of Jesus, the disciples had been stifled by fear and despair. Then came the post–resurrection promise about Galilee, and unparalleled enthusiasm and optimism erupted among them.

No doubt, during the long hours of Jesus' entombment, some of the disciples had discussed how they could ever preach and teach again. What would they say? Already some men in this fellowship were probably stating their intention to return to the sea and to start fishing again. But all of that changed when they heard Jesus' summons to Galilee. How could they ever again be quiet about Jesus? Not only had He told them what to do immediately, He had promised to be there as they obeyed—"He is going to Galilee."

Within the Galilee–related commission from Jesus is substantive promise for us as well. Even when sharing the gospel seems to be a waste of time, when the message of salvation sounds senseless, when listeners laugh at a call to morality—it is all worthwhile. We must not quit. When a witness about Christ seems unwelcome or when words about Jesus seem to fall on deaf ears, we must not give up. Jesus is in all of that talk because Jesus is in Galilee. Comments about Jesus and His ethics will not pass away, the words of Jesus will last forever.

Ordinary acts of helpfulness become extraordinary means of ministry because of Christ's presence. Jesus is in Galilee. Jesus is with us. His ministries in Galilee include visiting the sick, talking with the troubled, feeding the hungry, freeing the oppressed, loving the imprisoned, witnessing to the lost, and teaching the uneducated. Jesus is a part of all those activities. He is with us in Galilee.

Jesus is in Galilee. He is with us. An informal word about faith shared with a business associate, encouragement in a class of preschoolers, a shared moment with a person who is lonely——these are activities of inestimable importance. Jesus is in all such services.

The message from God's representative in the empty garden tomb is for everyone. Jesus is going before us. A meeting place has been arranged. We can join Jesus. His invitation is for everybody. That is why we are commissioned to share this invitation, to become a colleague with the heavenly messenger. Even while we move to accept the invitation of Jesus, we obey the commission from Jesus. Even as we are making our way to and through Galilee, we are telling the story of the resurrected Lord to all whom we meet.

The messenger from God who met the two women in Jesus' tomb shared the earth–shaking truth of the resurrection with the women. These women passed that explosive message along to the disciples. The Gospels writers Mark and Matthew passed this overwhelming truth along to us. "He is going to Galilee."

Galilee. That is the meeting place.

Scurrying around and throwing things together to head out on a journey to Galilee to meet the risen Christ, the truth of the Scriptures stops us in our tracks. *Galilee is here!* Our already–pounding hearts beat even faster. The news seems too good to be true. Galilee is where we live. Standing in Galilee, we see and understand the resurrection–oriented truth as never before.

Galilee is a place of invitation. We are invited to meet Jesus right where we live. Galilee is a place of commission. We are mandated to serve Jesus right where we work, rest, worship, and play.

Jesus is risen from the dead. He lives. He is here. We can meet Christ daily in Galilee.

21

EMMAUS:
A GIVING-UP PLACE

two . . . were going . . . to a village named Emmaus . . . .
While they were conversing and discussing together, Jesus
Himself approached, and began traveling with them.
— Luke 24:13, 15

E XASPERATED BY THE LACK OF cooperation he
receives from Lucy, Charlie Brown, the beloved cartoon character created by Charles Schultz, asks,
"Where do you go to give up?"[1] The same question crosses the
lips of a woman discouraged by the apparent failure of her best
efforts at parenting and a man who watches the dissolution of
a long-standing business relationship. No cartoons here,
though. This is real life.

"Where do you go to give up?" is what people ask who have
done everything they know to do to solve a problem—and who

learn that their efforts are not enough. Commonly the question is raised with a sigh of resignation and no expectation of an answer. The inquiry is actually a form of declaration—"I've had it! I'm finished. I quit."—coming from a person who has decided to drop out of life, but isn't quite sure how to do it.

Emmaus! The word resounds like an echo every time the "where do you go to give up" question is asked. "Emmaus" is the answer to Charlie Brown's inquiry—and to the inquiries of the troubled mother and the disturbed businessman and to my question or yours.

Emmaus is the giving–up place. When a dream has died or a vision has faded, people set out for Emmaus. This is the place which people seek when their savior has been killed, their future jeopardized, and their hopes robbed of all substance.

Each of these two followers must have had similar thoughts that day: *I want to believe the Easter truth. Rumors about it are rampant. Otherwise curious folks speak about the risen Christ with great excitement. I am tempted to accept what I hear. But, I saw him die. And I am a realist. Crucifixion is totally believable. But resurrection? I just don't know. Maybe I need to get away for a while. I think I will head toward Emmaus.*

A PLACE OF REFUGE

The giving–up place is never far from the problem place. According to Luke's Gospel, Emmaus was only seven miles from Jerusalem. Honestly, though, in the geography of the soul, the two places seem to be even closer to each other than that. However, Emmaus is far enough away from Jerusalem to make a difference. At least, at the giving–up place, the site of major difficulties is always somewhere else.

Just as the problem place is not always known as Jerusalem, the giving–up place is not always called Emmaus. Everyone has her own name for this kind of spot. Developments in school take a downward turn. A test is failed. A project is rejected. Pressure builds. The troubled student resolves, *I have got to get away.*

At the office, responsibilities have stacked up imposingly. Thinking he will be unable to accomplish everything prior to the deadline, an executive wants to run. The destination does not matter. He rubs the ache in the back of his tension–hardened neck and mumbles to himself, *I must get away from here at least for a while.*

For some people, the place they want to get away from is the place they call home. The marriage is not going well. Relationships with the children are rough. An emotionally–over–extended mother realizes that her energy is totally depleted. The only alternative she can see is diversion, maybe by way of distance. The young woman starts to ponder how she will break her news to the rest of the family, *Right now, I cannot stay here any longer. I have got to go somewhere else for a time.*

Each of these situations can send a person scrambling toward Emmaus—running breathlessly to arrive at a giving–up place. For some folks, it is a hide–out—a place to be alone, a location unknown to other family members, friends, and acquaintances. Emmaus can be a library, a theater, a grassy meadow, a racetrack, a deserted beach, or any one of thousands of other places—some likely to help, others likely to compound the problems of the person seeking a giving-up place.

Emmaus is the spot which a man seeks in the midst of a mid–life crisis. Emmaus is the place pursued when a person feels under stress. A desire to find Emmaus accompanies a loss of joy. When life no longer seems to have any purpose, when injustice and unfairness appear to be the only absolutes in which a person can trust, when a bad situation needs to be put in the past—people take off in the direction of Emmaus. Emmaus is the giving–up place.

The Sunday after the crucifixion of Jesus was for His disciples what an incredibly bad Monday is for many people today and more. Jesus died on Friday. Followers of Jesus were badly hurt. But Saturday had always been a special day. The Sabbath was set aside for rest, silence, and worship. They needed that. Then came Sunday, though. Sunday was different. For the disciples, Sunday was the day to get back to their routines, to give themselves to ordinary tasks which required their attention, if they could even remember such tasks in their bereaved state. Sunday morning was the time when life was supposed to get started again.

With the dawn of this particular Sunday morning came devastating realizations which broad sided their emotions and tore at their security: *Jesus is dead! We must get up and go on with our lives without the One whom we have learned to call "Lord." The Messiah for whom we left everything and everyone else has now left us.* It was more than some of the men could take. At least two of Jesus' followers decided that they had to get out of town. That very day they started walking toward Emmaus.

Along the way, Jesus joined their journey. An immediate benefit of the resurrection was an ever–present Christ. Getting out of Jerusalem was not the same as getting away from Jesus.

Jesus recognized their despondency. He understood their confusion and disorientation, disappointment and hurt. Mentally and emotionally, they were torn between belief in the resurrection rumors and coping with the crucifixion reality.

Jesus came to be with them—not to reprimand them for insufficient faith, not to judge them for seeking to get away, not to lecture them never to give up on anything or anybody, not to admonish them to lift their chins and think positively. Jesus just came to be with them. Jesus joins people even when they are headed toward a giving–up place.

The Emmaus road travelers did not recognize Jesus immediately. That is no surprise; we cannot hold it against them. Sometimes Jesus goes unrecognized even among people who believe in the resurrection and have the benefit of two thousand years of testimony regarding its reality. These men *were not looking* for Jesus. Their minds had changed rapidly. Jesus was mentioned in their conversation, but only as "a prophet." No contemporary would have second-guessed their reasoning. *If Jesus had been the Messiah, He would not have died. No doubt He was only one more man in a long line of prophets—a good one to be sure, superior to His predecessors, but still a prophet, nothing more. We need to face the fact: Jesus is dead.*

Thankfully, the reality of Christ's presence is not dependent upon human judgment. Help from Christ is not contingent upon a quick recognition of Christ—then or now. Jesus joined these two disciples as they plodded toward a giving–up place. He was their partner and friend, still their Savior, though they did not know it.

Jesus is always doing something like that—showing up unexpectedly, maybe even incognito. We do not ever walk completely alone—not really, not even when it seems like that is the case. Jesus joins our journeys whether we are going toward Jerusalem or headed in the opposite direction, whether we are on our way to accept an exciting challenge or looking for a means of quitting everything.

A PLACE OF PERSPECTIVE

As Jesus walked along with the two sad disciples, He provided a much-needed perspective on their predicament. Things were not precisely as these men thought. The two men were traveling with a half-truth, running away from a gospel much more complete than they imagined. Confusion reigned, and grief caused a loss of sight. The journeymen did not know what really was going on. Jesus was not threatened by their situation or angered by it. He continued to walk with them and in the process ministered to them exactly at the point of their misunderstanding.

Jesus allowed the two disciples to talk and to express their feelings. In fact, He asked leading questions aimed at drawing out the deepest concerns of these travelers. It did not take much prodding before disappointment and anger gushed forth.

The unrecognized Jesus was the object of their initial outburst. "Are you the only visitor in Jerusalem who doesn't know what has been happening there during the past several days?" they asked. "How could you have missed such important news?" That was all right—the strange words and the indignant attitude.

Jesus wanted to hear precisely what they said. Jesus wanted to hear what was on the inside of these men, to hear why they were so intent on giving up. Occasionally Jesus inserted a word about resurrection into a conversation which was dominated by references to the crucifixion. Mostly, though, He just allowed the travelers to talk.

When, finally, the two men fell silent, Jesus began to interpret the events which had dominated their attention and discussion. He made use of the Scriptures—which all three of them knew well—to set the recent happenings in their proper context. In a very compassionate manner, Jesus said to His fellow travelers, "Don't be too hasty in your judgments. You need to look again at this whole situation. Reality is not exactly as you perceive it."

As Jesus talked, things changed. To their amazement, Jesus pointed out how the Scriptures had anticipated as potentially good the very actions which these two despondent men had dubbed as totally evil. What they had perceived as the end of everything, God intended as a radical new beginning.

How indescribably helpful it is when Jesus does something like this. Often a new perspective is the very best corrective to a situation in which giving–up proceedings have begun. People get so engrossed in what they are doing in their own little worlds that they lose sight of the larger picture. Work seems like the only activity of any significance. One estranged relationship threatens to ruin a person's entire existence. A really bad day takes on the proportions of a totally bad life. Perspective—a different and more honest perspective—is needed. Jesus always helps us see life accurately.

In the present as in the past, the Bible is a major source of assistance. When heading out for a giving–up place, the Bible is an excellent book to take along. Studied under the tutelage of Christ, the Scriptures can nurture a healthy perspective on life. Temporary setbacks can be distinguished from an ultimate defeat. One period of hurt can be endured without forming the conclusion that all of life consists of pain. Suffering can be seen as a way to God rather than as an experience which stands apart from God. Jesus encourages sensitivity to the truths of the Scriptures and enables people—even profoundly troubled people—to set their experiences within the context of God's will.

A PLACE OF TRUTH

Jesus stayed with the two Emmaus road travelers until they arrived at their giving–up place. God creates people to be free and allows individuals to go wherever their wills take them. These men arrived in Emmaus.

At last! The two fatigued men breathed a sigh of relief. Finally they had put distance between themselves and the city in which their highest hopes had been dashed. Now they could enjoy a meal outside Jerusalem. Maybe they would be able to taste food again and to swallow without feeling that every bite was going to lodge in their throats.

What irony! At the very moment and place when the two runaway disciples surmised they were farther removed from recent problems than they had been for days, they were closer to all of it than they had ever been before. But what they faced was no problem. Jesus was there. Jesus was with them. Jesus was in Emmaus.

Suddenly the truth hit them. Outside the room in which these two men sat talking, the sun was sinking below the horizon at day's end. However, in their lives it was sunrise, a new day, a new life. Jesus was with them. They finally had reached the giving–up place and there—incredibly, there!— they had encountered the Christ.

Quickly the pieces of the puzzle began to fall into place. No wonder the two had experienced such a strange, inexplicable burning sensation in their spirits. Jesus had been with them the whole day. While they were running away, Jesus had run toward them and then with them. All that they needed was available to them right where they were.

Often it happens that way. We reach the end of our ropes. Life gets as bad as it can get. Hurt is as deep as it can ever go.

Anxieties are as heavy as anyone can carry. Giving up seems to be the only possible decision that can be made. Nothing else makes sense. We give up. Then it happens. There, of all places, right there—where everything seems to be ending—Jesus is discovered. Patiently, lovingly, the Lord allows us to recognize His presence. There is nowhere else to go and no one else to whom to turn. But Jesus is there. Jesus is here. Jesus invites us to turn to Him.

At one time or another, everyone senses the need to travel, physically or emotionally, to a giving–up place. When that occurs, such a development does not deserve to be condemned. Most likely it is a predictable component of the human condition.

Jesus is present at the giving–up place; thus, alternatives exist even there. Plagued by difficulties, people can give up, quit, be done with everything, walk away from all that is known, opt for despair. God will permit that choice. But it doesn't have to be that way. Another option is to give up purposefully, to surrender everything to the One who is there, to entrust life to Christ. God invites such action.

Jesus joins us where we are—wherever we are. He walks with us whether our steps take us through the streets of Jerusalem or along the road to Emmaus. Jesus does not forsake us—not ever, whether we are doing just fine, barely surviving, or giving up.

What happened to the two despairing disciples *after* they met the risen Christ? Their day had started early. By evening they were very tired. They would be late getting back to Jerusalem, but that was precisely where they were going. Emmaus was not the place for them on this night. They were not giving up. The two road–weary travelers made their way straight back to the city in which their difficulties had begun.

Once there, they breathlessly sought out other disciples and joyfully exposed the reason for their return, for the burning in their hearts, "Jesus is risen indeed!"

Words first heard in whispered rumors were now shouted as fact. These two men had met Jesus. He had found them and joined their journey. Jesus had walked with them to the very spot where they intended to escape. Jesus loved them even though they were ready to quit everything. As a result, the two men *had* given up, but not as they originally intended. They had given up to Jesus. Certainty pervaded their confessions: "Jesus is risen. Jesus is Lord."

Here is a promise of the highest order for all people. If we can keep it in focus, we may never embark on a pilgrimage to a giving–up place. The presence of Jesus is real even if not visible. We are never alone. Jesus is always available.

But the fact is that we do not keep this truth in focus. At times our minds grow weary and our emotions dull. We forget. We can see no resources beyond our own abilities. We can hear no words other than the whispers of our own pessimism. We get to the point where we have had enough. Trying to set it all behind us, we begin looking for a place to quit. That is all right. Jesus is with us at that moment also.

If we do not stop before the journey to the giving–up place is completed—and we actually arrive at a place where we feel we can be done with life—Jesus will be there too. Jesus takes people at their worst with the same love He extends when people are at their best. At the giving–up place, Jesus will invite us to give up to Him, an experience which is better understood as receiving everything than giving up anything.

This Emmaus reality is strange but true. Sometimes it seems too good to be true, but that is not the case. We walk toward a sunset, and rays of the rising sun hit us in the face. In the midst of despair, we stumble on joyful hope. Finally arriving at the giving–up place, we meet the One who gives us all we need never to give up.

What great good news! And so much for walking to Emmaus. I cannot keep from running there myself.

NOTES

Acknowledgments

1. Alfred Edersheim, *The Life and Times of Jesus the Messiah,* two volumes (Grand Rapids, MI: Wm. B. Eerdmans Publishing Company, 1947).

2. George Arthur Buttrick, ed., *The Interpreter's Dictionary of the Bible,* four volumes (Nashville: Abingdon Press, 1962).

Chapter 5

1. William Barclay, *The Gospel of Matthew,* vol. 1 (Philadelphia: The Westminster Press, 1958), 56.

2. Wayne E. Oates, *Convictions That Give You Confidence* (Philadelphia: The Westminster Press, 1984), 35.

Chapter 12

1. Conrad Hyers, *An God Created Laughter: The Bible as Divine Comedy* (Atlanta: John Knox Press, 1987), 79–80, citing George

Bernard Shaw, *Saint Joan* (Indianapolis, IN: Bobbs-Merrill, 1971), 113.

Chapter 21

1. I have detailed a description of this Charles Schultz cartoon in a book with the title inspired by the inquiry from Charlie Brown. C. Welton Gaddy, *Where Do You Go To Give Up? Building a Community of Grace* (Macon, GA: Smyth & Helwys Publishing, Inc., 1993).